Sex Is God's Idea

Ⓚ

Earl Paulk

Copyright 1985
K-Dimension Publishers
Atlanta, Georgia

Printed in the United States of America
ISBN 0-917595-04-1

DEDICATION

To my granddaughter, Penielle Brook Bonner, and all the other "truth seekers" in her generation.

May the Truth of the Kingdom of God concerning every area of life give you freedom from oppressive darkness and prepare the maturing Bride of Christ to rule and reign forever with the King.

ACKNOWLEDGEMENTS

I want to thank the Publications Department of Chapel Hill Harvester Church for their daily efforts and faithfulness to the Lord in making this book possible.

I especially thank Tricia Weeks for diligent oversight and direction in rewriting and editing these manuscripts.

I sincerely appreciate the contributions of members of our Editorial Staff: Chris Oborne, Gail Smith and Gayle Blackwood.

For all the technical aspects of publishing this book, I thank Wes Bonner. A special thanks to Don Ross for layout and paste-up, Wayne Henderson for word processing, and Donna Eubanks for typesetting.

Finally, I am grateful for faithful volunteers, Kae Rivenbark and Angela Hamrick, who gave their time and skills to the Lord in assisting in the Publications Department.

May the seeds of these words bear much fruit to the glory of Christ's Kingdom.

TABLE OF CONTENTS

PAGE

TABLE OF CONTENTS

1

THE KINGDOM OF SEX

God is no dummy about sex. The deception that says "sex is evil" does not lift people to a higher dimension of life. It is the misuse of sex which is evil. A gleeful Satan has taken sex from the arms of the Church and has used it effectively to merchandise his philosophy that self-gratification insures a happy life. Satan uses sex to sell everything from cars to handkerchiefs. Meanwhile, all the Church says about sex is one big word: NO!

Satan uses a sexual mentality to promote his cause in entertainment, food, clothing and almost every other industry. The Bible is filled with examples of sexuality's influence used for both good and evil purposes. Satan used the sexuality of Salome to cause Herod to behead John the Baptist. He used Jezebel to control King Ahab in challenging the prophet Elijah. He attempted to overthrow David and the kingdom of Israel through David's affair with Bathsheba.

Isn't it about time we realized that not only was sex God's idea, but God also used sex to influence kingdoms and to change lives for good? Nothing less than a combination of obedience and sexuality gave Esther half the kingdom and saved the Jews from destruction. The literal meaning of Paul's exhortation to wives in I Corinthians 7 was for them to use sex as a tool to bring their unbelieving husbands to accept the way of life in Christ. If any kingdom needs to be reclaimed by the Church and properly understood, it is the kingdom of sex.

God's one, consoling promise to the man and woman when He cursed their disobedience in the Garden of Eden was that through "the (fertilized) seed of the woman," God would "crush the head" of the serpent (Genesis 3:15). While this promise was clearly Messianic and refers specifically to the divine conception of Jesus by the Holy Spirit, God's promise extended through human conception for many generations of His people and through that conception, gave hope of God's redemption to the fallen human race. God intended our sexuality to be a life-giving, renewing experience in many dimensions of our lives: spiritually, emotionally and physically.

When I first began teaching a series on Christian sexuality to my congregation at Chapel Hill Harvester

2

Church in Atlanta, I had no idea of the tremendous response that this series would generate. Our tape department was unprepared at that time to handle the increased demand for tapes after each session. Hundreds of people who heard the teaching were purchasing tapes for themselves as well as for family and friends—many who were not Christians—who needed the ministry of truth in this sensitive area of their lives.

After the first session, I began receiving many letters from people whose lives were being changed dramatically. They shared with me how the truth had begun to confront so many harmful patterns insidiously influencing their daily thinking and behavior. Many testimonies confirmed that the confrontation of inner darkness with God's truth was beginning to expose hidden corners in their thoughts and attitudes. They began to understand some of their lifelong, emotional problems which their parents may have unintentionally passed on to them. Others were beginning to open dialogue in their marriages that surfaced both frustrations and appreciation which in some cases had never been verbally expressed. When people are spiritually open and receptive to truth, they are always set free from bondages.

By the time the "Christian Sexuality" series was broadcast on our national PTL satellite program, K-DIMENSION MAGAZINE, our publications staff had begun transcribing the teaching series for this book. Again, the television response from our audience was overwhelming. Great numbers of people were calling from across the country during and after each broadcast. Mail, commenting favorably on the series and ordering tapes, flooded our **Partners For the Kingdom** offices for months after we aired the final program of the series.

Having been a pastor for forty years, I was not at all surprised by the need for this teaching in people's lives. I was encouraged, however, to discover the numbers of people who were diligently searching for direct answers to God's will for enjoying a fulfilling sexual relationship. Many parents expressed gratitude for the honesty of the series in offering them guidelines to foster healthy sexual identities in their children.

We live in a day of obsessively brazen sexuality, yet misinformation and distorted attitudes on this subject abound in our society. Unfortunately, the Church has been either too evasive or too rigid in offering teaching which defines sexuality according to God's purposes. I realize that many of the subjects discussed in this book could offend some readers. In spite of that realization, I refuse to back away from the bold candor of its content. A modest discussion of Christian sexuality may benefit some segments of the Church and our society, but the majority of people with problems related to sex must grope vainly for answers from sources far removed from godly counsel. For the most part, the Church still refuses to address real issues in specific areas of personal needs.

Every person is a sexual being. This common thread of expression in all people has the power to greatly influence us far beyond our conscious realization. The desire for a good sexual image is intrinsic in our responses to advertising as well as being an essential factor in maintaining a personal sense of identity and well being. Every person desires acceptance. We all need to be needed. We need to love and be loved; to understand and be understood. We have a desire to "fit" into our culture and society.

Social, sexual values influence our means of fulfilling these highly motivated desires within us. A Christian in our society faces a major, cultural conflict in developing attitudes that please God in a fulfilling, sexual relationship. Current social attitudes are often distorted and extreme. God's will is lost in a tug-of-war between the extreme attitudes of "playboy/playgirl propensity" on one side and a strong adherence to "Victorian suppression" on the other. Somewhere between two social extremes is sexual intimacy as God intended it to be.

The "playboy" philosophy of human sexuality disregards the fact that God created sex and called it "good." This philosophy flaunts sexuality at the Church like naughty children who willfully insist on disobeying the rules at school. Unfortunately, the Church too often has played the role of a strict schoolmaster in this moral scenario—frowning on all suggestions that sex is indeed a very beautiful, pleasurable, acceptable means of communication between a man and a woman.

The other extreme in social, sexual values is an oppressive "Victorian" regard for sexuality in which people try to hide a normal experience of human life which is undeniably obvious. An oppressive view of sexuality undermines any healthy view of the subject by implying that sexual intimacy is necessary to produce children, but any other reason is sinful, risque and taboo. Too many Christians live their entire lives in emotional bondages which produce guilt. Unfortunately, the Church has traditionally commended suppression because it maintains behavior codes which appear to be "spiritual."

As a young pastor who was called into the ministry at the age of seventeen, I can remember my dad, a great Pentecostal pastor, saying to me, "If you ever touch a woman, your ministry is over!" I lived years of my life in complete adherence to a rigid morality which was devoid of any expressions of compassion or tenderness. Fear ruled my emotions. My pharisaic morals caused me to be a strict disciplinarian and a harsh judge of others who would "fall into sin." Inside an emotional prison, I was so threatened by the possibility of "wrong" feelings that even proper, approved relationships were strained at times under tremendous convictions that I must "deny the flesh."

My impeccable moral standards were controlled by the expectations of the Church and society. Only years later through a series of devastating circumstances did I begin to comprehend that God's desires in Christian relationships are demonstrated in the example of Jesus Christ. Jesus loved people with a freedom and purity that accepted them wherever they were in their lives and lifted them to a higher, purer realm. He loved women as well as other men. He was touchable and physically expressive. He had no fear of being close to people and allowed them to express their affections to Him openly in spite of criticism from "religious" leaders.

Jesus deliberately broke moral codes of His day to love and minister to certain people. He probably even confused His disciples with His bold conversation with the Samaritan woman at the well who was "living with" her latest (at least number six) boyfriend (John 4). His virtue healed a woman with an issue of blood when the Mosaic law forbade a man to touch her (Mark 5:25-30). His disciples were certainly not the type of men the Church would normally ordain as pastors: unscrupulous businessmen (Matthew 21:31) and burly fishermen with crude language and unrefined manners.

Jesus used certain metaphors to identify Himself with the sexuality of both men and women. He called Himself a "Bridegroom" in expressing the passionate intensity of His love for those who followed Him (Mark 9:15, Matthew 25:1). He is undoubtedly the "Father" in the parable of the prodigal son (Luke 15:11-32). He wept over Jerusalem and said He felt like a "mother hen" who wanted to gather "her" chicks to "herself" (Matthew 23:37). He identifies Himself with a woman having a baby in describing the crucifixion He faced by saying, ". . . **she** has sorrow, because **her** hour has come; but as soon as **she** has given birth to the child, **she** no longer remembers the anguish. . ." (John 16:21).

After examining Jesus' relationships closely, we realize that the most radical commission in the Bible is the one Jesus gave to His disciples, "Love one another as I have loved you" (John 15:12). Why then has the Church lost the example of Jesus' love in developing relationships? Why have we allowed society to dictate morality to people who are born of the Spirit and have the "mind" of Jesus Christ? How could we miss demonstrating Paul's comparison of the love between a husband and wife as an earthly relationship reflecting the love between Christ and the Church?

The time has come for the Church to offer alternatives to the world which has so flagrantly maligned sexuality as God intended it to be. God's ways bring life to people while Satan always destroys any possibility of fulfillment or purpose. All around us are people whose lives are wounded and whose spirits are broken because Satan's enticing kingdom of sex has trapped them in some situation or relationship in which they begin to topple in a downward spiral from God's perfect will for their lives.

God created the desire for intimacy within us. The desire for close fellowship is characteristic of God Himself and we are created in His image. Satan exploits the innate desire for intimacy with promises of fulfillment without a committed relationship. Satan focuses our attention on "getting" instead of "sharing" physical pleasure with a chosen covenant partner. Sex becomes a method of self-gratification and selfish exploitation of others.

The most viable alternative to Satan's kingdom of sex is training our children from their earliest years to value their bodies as God's creation and to build solid, loving relationships with others. We must teach them,

8

"There is no fear in love, but perfect love casts out fear
. . ." (I John 4:18). Perfect love is spiritual, godly love
that flows from the Holy Spirit within us. The fruit of
God's perfect love is always righteousness, peace and
joy in our relationships. What a contrast between the
righteousness, peace and joy characterizing Kingdom
love and the exploitive lusts of worldly sexuality!

If the Church awakens to challenge the worldly
kingdom of sex with God's alternatives, where do we
begin? Must we simply wait for a new generation to
grow up without having to fight through all our own
social "hang-ups" and mistaken concepts? No, I
believe that the Church can now become that "City of
Refuge" to those who are hopelessly trapped by forces
and controlling powers in the kingdom of sex.

Christ in us is greater than all evil powers and principalities. His deliverance is available today to those
who call upon Him. Through His power of deliverance
in anointed ministries, God empowers His people to
take dominion and thwart all attempts by the kingdom
of sex to destroy lives.

In 1960 God gave me a vision of a church which
would become a City of Refuge to those who were seeking a new start in their lives. Through prayer, claiming
God's Word and close relationships, I have seen hundreds of people restored from devastating circumstances which seemed to be totally hopeless. I look across
my congregation at the faces of people as they worship
the Lord. Many lives are filled with abundance beyond
all that anyone could ask or think because they chose
to trust God in a crisis. Whatever hope is offered in this

9

book is documented in the lives of many people I have loved and known personally as their pastor. God keeps His promises to those who believe in Him.

Chapel Hill Harvester Church has many ministries which are dedicated to setting people free from bondages in their lives. The proof of God's power is in the fruit of these ministries. I want to share some testimonies of people from these ministries who are dedicated specifically to challenging the worldly kingdom of sex. These people are living examples whom God has raised up as witnesses against Satan's destructive ploys intended to steal, kill and destroy lives.

Fred and Sandy Cassidy bought a huge two-story house near our church in 1980 and moved in with their four children, all under six years of age. The upstairs became the family living quarters and the downstairs became a dormitory for seven unwed, pregnant girls (I hesitate to call them "women" since some have been as young as fourteen years old).

Fred, a successful businessman, and Sandy, an outspoken dynamo with a great sense of humor, are the resident "daddy and mother" and counselors to young girls and their families who are experiencing a time in their lives which seems like a traumatic nightmare.

These girls live at the *House of New Life* as members of the Cassidy family until their babies are born. They prepare family meals served at a huge, wooden, dining room table. They go to doctors' appointments and to church in the Cassidys' passenger van. Many of these girls experience life in a Christian home for the first time in their lives during their pregnancies.

Each girl is assigned a labor support "mother" from volunteers in our church who walk with the girl through the final months of her pregnancy: childbirth classes; the labor room and delivery experience; and finally, the adoption of her baby to a Christian couple through our church's adoption ministry, *In His Care,* if she makes that choice.

The Cassidys don't just talk against abortion; they offer an alternative. Why? Both Fred and Sandy have painful memories from their own teen years. They remember feeling trapped and scared and not knowing where to turn for help. Because of their own experience they understand why kids make the wrong choices and get into desperate trouble.

When Jesus releases people from guilt, they always experience freedom and gratitude, and some of them even give something priceless back to Him. Shortly after Fred and Sandy made commitments to Jesus Christ and joined our church, the idea for *House of New Life* was born in Fred's heart. He came to my office and shared with me the concept for *House of New Life.* I agreed with Fred that together we would pray and seek God's will, and perhaps God would open doors for this ministry. Within a few weeks the Cassidys opened their home to their first, young, pregnant girl who lived with them until her baby was born.

After submitting the things God had spoken to them and getting the final blessing from the Presbytery of Chapel Hill Harvester Church, Fred and Sandy sold their beautiful home in a prestigious part of the county to purchase the *House of New Life,* a house easily converted into a "boardinghouse" dwelling.

Fred and Sandy are the kind of people who will walk two miles if someone asks them to walk one. They would give both their coats and their cloaks if someone were cold and asked them for a sweater. They adopted a sixteen-year-old from south Georgia after she had come to the *House of New Life* to have a baby daughter whom she gave to the Lord in adoption. She became the Cassidys' oldest, fifth child.

The logo for *House of New Life* is a butterfly. Many beautiful, young women have struggled out of a prison-like cocoon through the transforming power of God. Today many of these women have gone back to school, gotten jobs, and settled into life in our community as responsible, contributing adults with talents they are using for God.

"New Life" is not an empty promise to many young women who come in desperation to a church called to be a City of Refuge. I have performed wedding ceremonies for many of them who have become members of my church during their pregnancies, and met their husbands here. Many of these women (following Fred and Sandy Cassidy's example) are now actively involved in ministries serving others.

Another ploy of Satan's kingdom of sex causes divorce with all the devastation it can bring. Sometimes even Christian families are torn in this mighty struggle. Sharon Price is a petite brunette with a beautiful smile who looks more like an older sister than mother to her married son and two teenaged daughters. Sharon is a spiritual life-giver: warm, loving and powerfully effective in helping others see God's goodness in any circumstance. She is an intercessor and worshipper who lives the words she prays.

Sharon came to Chapel Hill after the most painful divorce that a woman who considers herself to be "happily married" can experience. Her husband's unfaithfulness was complicated by the fact that they had served in a well-known, evangelistic ministry for many years and were pastors of a thriving Pentecostal church. Sharon had sung, played the organ, and flowed in the Spirit with her husband's powerful preaching since she was nineteen years old. Now everything seemed to be over: the ministry, life-long security, and the relationship she had cherished.

I met with Sharon in my office shortly after she joined our church. Beneath all the pain of the past and the unanswered questions about the future, Sharon glowed with an inner peace and confidence in the Lord. I recognized how much her heart was drawn toward serving in the ministry.

A few weeks later at a Wednesday night service at our church, the Lord spoke to me as I sat on the platform waiting to preach. He told me to ask Sharon to join our staff. I shared with my brother, Don, what God had spoken to my spirit about Sharon, and he gave me spiritual confirmation. Our congregation was exploding in growth, and so I asked Sharon to serve as our full-time receptionist. For several years Sharon was the first contact many people had with our ministry. Her warmth and love lifted everyone who walked through the door—other staff included—and her voice over the telephone exuded empathy and understanding that well represented the "heart" of Chapel Hill.

In 1982 I asked Sharon to lead *Hebron*, our singles ministry. She was very reluctant at first because (as she put it) she didn't "feel single." But as she began to work with a very talented Hebron planning committee and they creatively put together their monthly "events" as well as informal after-church gatherings, the dormant seeds of ministry inside Sharon suddenly burst and began to grow.

Hebron is now a vibrant ministry with several hundred members, and Sharon is a very busy lady. She is surrounded by many people who come to *Hebron* with great needs, many times in circumstances similar to those which Sharon experienced. Out of the unlimited Source in her spirit, she is able to give peace, hope and assurance to those who are ready to give up and feel that their broken lives are beyond restoration. Sharon is proof that out of the ashes of circumstances which could so easily stir up bitterness and anger toward God, one who continues to trust Him will know a refreshing new plan which is both fulfilling and life-restoring.

I performed the wedding ceremony for Bob and Marie Middleton in November, 1981, on the day before Thanksgiving. That holiday was an appropriate time to begin this marriage for many reasons. A few years earlier, Marie had moved to Atlanta with her two little girls after a traumatic divorce. She taught English and drama at a local high school and in her strong commitment to the Lord, she began giving the drama ministry at Chapel Hill the full benefit of all her training and leadership abilities.

Bob Middleton attended the Kingdom Players' practices out of an interest in theater production. Over a period of time, Bob and Marie developed a close, trusting friendship. No one was surprised when that friendship began to bloom into a tender relationship which grew progressively more serious.

Bob's marriage to Marie was a major defeat to strong powers in Satan's kingdom of sex. Bob first came to our church with a group of men who were Christians, but still openly defensive of their homosexual lifestyle. I was very aware of their presence in our church services. The Lord instructed me to love and accept them among us, and He would correct the errors in their thinking so that they could be completely set free.

Whenever I would use scriptures related to homosexuality in the content of the messages I preached, God would move strongly in my spirit to avoid any condemnation of that lifestyle by focusing on "restoration" and "new beginnings" through Jesus Christ's liberating power. Bob Middleton and a few other men responded to the teaching by renouncing homosexuality in their lives. They submitted themselves totally to the authority of the church.

Now Bob and Marie lead *Such Were Some of You* each Friday night. This powerful ministry is provided for those wishing to come out of the homosexual community. *Such Were Some of You* (I Corinthians 6:9-11) also includes ministry to family members who are needing counseling to cope with the choices of relatives in bondage to homosexuality. Many times people drive for miles from distant cities to receive the hope and restoration that Christ gives through these meetings.

In addition to their full-time professional careers, Bob and Marie give hours each week in individual counseling and ministry of inner healing to those who want and need help against seductive spirits destroying their self-esteem. The love and happiness of their marriage—as well as the vital ministry God has called Bob and Marie to share with others—indeed has become as a prophecy over this couple proclaimed "a sword in Satan's side."

Bettye Anne Miles is an optimist whose sunny disposition can soothe any storm. She is one of those people who always has a "good" word in any situation and can brighten up a room the second she walks in the door. And why not? God has blessed Bettye Anne. She is a tall, attractive blond, happily married with two beautiful daughters. She is also an extremely competent executive secretary. A person gets the impression that someone as positive as Bettye Anne has never had to face any major conflicts in her life. No one with that radiant smile and up-beat music in her voice could possibly know that real life also has a tragic, somber side.

The truth is that Bettye Anne Miles lives daily as an overcoming witness against hell's most violent, abusive spirits. These spirits use the pent-up emotions in unstable people to attack others who are innocent and defenseless. Bettye Anne and her friend, Jean Buice, were having lunch in a park near the bank where they worked on a warm, fall day. As they were getting into the car to leave, the women were approached by two men who held them at gunpoint. The men took their purses, and then almost as an afterthought, they instructed the two women to walk to a secluded area of the woods where they were told to undress.

When Jean began to resist the threats and refused to cooperate, one of the men became very violent. Both women were tied up with their pantyhose, severely beaten, sexually assaulted and then left lying on the ground since both were supposedly dead. By a miracle in God's sovereignty, Bettye Anne regained consciousness. As she struggled to stand up, the binding simply fell off her wrists to the ground. She untied her feet, miraculously climbed a six-foot fence and ran to a nearby house to get help.

I rushed to the hospital as soon as Bettye Anne's husband telephoned me. When I walked into the hospital room, I hardly recognized her. Bettye Anne's face was badly bruised and swollen. She managed to smile, and in a typical "Bettye Anne" understatement, she said, "I don't think I'm going to make my Bible class tonight."

The following months were extremely difficult for Bettye Anne, her husband and their family. Her friend, Jean, died in the park, and Bettye Anne survived as the key witness in a sensationlized assault and murder trial. Many people in our community insisted on making the tragedy a major racial issue since the assailants were black men and the women were white. To help Bettye Anne deal with the racial overtones of the assault, I immediately sent Dr. Kirby Clements, a black pastor on our staff, to visit her in the hospital and to minister Christ's healing love to her.

Bettye Anne repeatedly and publicly re-lived the scene in the park in graphic details. I was amazed at the tremendous strength and power in her soft-spoken manner and fearless testimony. Everyone in the courtroom was visibly affected by her supernatural grace and gentleness. Even the hard-nosed press who were covering the trial were amazed at her courage.

Our church surrounded Bettye Anne and her family with restoring love and a place of peaceful refuge. She later described the ministry of love from the pastorate and people as being a true representation of Christ's body: His arms reaching out to embrace her; His legs running to meet whatever needs she had; His voice always speaking words of encouragement and faith. The strong stand that this ministry has always taken against racial prejudice defused many of those trying to exploit the racial aspects of the assault. But much credit for her restoration goes to Bettye Anne herself who remained open and receptive to those ready to share the healing love of Jesus with her.

Bettye Anne had been volunteering in the television department of our church several months before the assault. After the trial, she quickly resumed her volunteer post. Within fifteen months after the assault, she left her job at the bank to give birth to her second daughter, ending "gossipy" speculation of the permanent extent of her physical injuries. She now works part-time on our staff in a major outreach ministry.

These testimonies may seem like extreme examples of those victimized by the worldly kingdom of sex, but unfortunately their experiences are not so rare. The notable difference in the positive daily flow of these lives, when compared to thousands of others like them who are bitter and confused, is their restorative relationship with Jesus Christ and the healing love of a church which believes in the reality of a "new start."

I often feel like the Apostle John in his heavenly vision who saw a group of people dressed in glowing white robes. He asked an angel standing by him who they were. The angel replied, "These are people who have come out of great tribulation . . ." Their garments which were once stained by sin, scandal and shame have been replaced by the pure righteousness of Jesus Christ. As their pastor, I look into their hearts. They stand blameless before God, giving no one the power to destroy them with accusations or memories from the past.

I so much believe in God's restorative power that at times I've taken risks to reach those who are in trouble or harming others as a result of destructive spirits controlling their minds and bodies. Seductive spirits are real. They are tormenting to the one under their control and they can never be fully satisfied. Many times they are less "sexual" than physically abusive and controlling.

19

The control of seductive spirits is very different from sins resulting from flesh desires. There is a difference between sexual involvement and sexual entanglement. David sinned in his adulterous desire for Bathsheba motivated by his passionate attraction to her physical beauty. David was not controlled by seductive spirits. His flesh desires were unsubmitted to God. The story of Delilah and Samson is another matter altogether. Delilah's actions are a classic example of seductive spirits at work. Delilah used her sexuality to destroy Samson's covenant with God. Sexuality became a means of pursuing control of Samson's power over his enemies.

People open to the occult, the drug culture, or environments of physical and mental abuse can entertain seductive spirits and become trapped by insidious distortions of their normal sexual drives. Depending on the strength of that person's own will and his desire to resist destructive mental and emotional impressions, the control of these spirits within people can become an absolutely ravaging, driving force.

Seductive spirits work through frustrated, confused individuals to manipulate their thoughts and actions. But these spirits also have the power to use their human channels to terrorize an entire city or even a nation. These spirits attack victims who are usually helpless, innocent, even trusting people. The current disclosures of rampant sexual abuse of children in day care centers are beginning to reveal the shocking extent and frequency of seductive spirits in our society. For almost three years, Atlanta was powerfully gripped in fear against seductive spirits terrorizing our children. A missing child always causes concern, but in Atlanta from July, 1979, to the early months of 1982, a missing child caused city-wide—and even nationwide—panic.

Like the parents in other families throughout our city, people in my congregation became obsessively protective of their children and deeply concerned about what they could do to end the horrifying tragedies. Families with young, black sons—the primary targets of the murders—were especially distraught under the constant threat hanging over their children's lives. Parents made strict rules about their children's activities, even forbidding them to play outdoors. The entire city was under a strict curfew for children in public places. Children were warned about trusting policemen, school officials, mail carriers and other public servants because the killer was thought to be someone whom they would not normally suspect as being malevolent.

I became involved in the missing and murdered children's cases as a spokesman from the Church at the request of the NAACP President, Dr. Frazier Ben Todd. On February 14, 1981, I made a television appeal at the end of our **Harvester Hour** program to the killer (or killers) after running an advertisement that morning in the *Atlanta Journal and Constitution*. The advertisement simply stated, "If you are responsible for the crimes against our children, This Television Appeal Is To You. Watch Saturday, February 14, Channel 46, 11:00 p.m."

21

In that five minute appeal to the "killer(s)," I offered myself to be directed by him (them) to a time and place where we could meet. I explained that though our community was undeniably suffering, I knew that the person responsible for the deaths of these children was also suffering inside and perhaps felt as if he couldn't control his actions. I assured him that the Church could minister to his needs and I believed God would forgive him and he could be restored. We also offered him a public platform to speak any grievances which he felt against society. Finally, I offered the church as a "safe" place to surrender to authorities. I assured him that we would provide physical protection so that he could end the assaults tormenting both our community and himself.

I began receiving calls from the supposed "killers" on February 15. Many of the calls were obvious hoaxes. Whether I ever actually spoke with the man convicted of the Atlanta child murders, I can't be sure. I am certain, however, based on the events that followed the television appeal, that my actions were a direct confrontation to powerful, seductive spirits over our city. The appeal definitely caught the attention of the actual killer since he left the next victim within one-fourth mile of our church.

On February 16, I began receiving a series of calls that never lasted more than ten to twenty seconds. The first call instructed me to go to a local television station in time for the 6:00 p.m. news broadcast. Nothing happened. I received a second call within hours from the same person instructing me to go to another television station for the 11:00 p.m. broadcast. Again, no call to the station, no message, nothing happened. At 11:30 a.m. the next day, the same man called to say that he was disappointed that I was not on camera during the broadcasts. I assured him that I had followed his instructions explicitly.

Meanwhile, a city-wide rally was held at our church on a Sunday afternoon at the request of the NAACP. I contended throughout the horrible ordeal terrorizing our city that the killings were motivated by seductive spirits rather than fanatical, racial prejudices as many people believed. Markings on some of the bodies indicating occult influences, as well as knowledge in my own spirit as I prayed about the matter, assured me that the warfare was sexually motivated. These spirits wanted to terrorize our city and control legal authorities. Our twenty-four hour, daily prayer vigil at our church continually prayed against these sexually aggressive spirits attacking our children.

I received another call—the same voice as previously—the day after the NAACP rally. I made another appeal to the killer on our own broadcast on February 28th. The last call I received from that same caller was three days before the twentieth victim, thirteen-year-old Curtis Walker, disappeared. The caller was very nervous that the telephone lines were tapped and that I was cooperating with authorities in setting a trap for him. Curtis Walker's partly-submerged body was found on March 6, caught on a log just off the bank of the South River which is adjacent to our church property—only one-fourth mile from the doors of our church.

The message was clear to me as well as to the media. *NBC Magazine* with David Brinkley covered the story of our appeals to the killer. Local news and national wire services also sent reporters to interview me to try to discover how the information we could give them might fit into the total puzzle of the crazed mind directing this elusive killer.

I felt somewhat exasperated and grieved by our well-intentioned involvement. I am sure that many people misunderstood the motives that would cause a pastor to open the doors of his church to a killer. I could think of no place more appropriate for him to end his own torment. I still wonder if the local law enforcement and the F.B.I. intervention in my sincere appeal to help the killer confess might have prolonged the series of deaths in Atlanta. I do know that during the time I was receiving calls, on a night when the voice said he would meet me, a van (which the caller had described over the telephone) drove slowly into the parking lot of a church across the street from ours. The van turned around and sped down the road. I later got another call, furiously accusing me of setting a trap for him. He said he had spotted patrol cars parked at a convenience store nearby.

I never intended to become a "trap" for the killer. I deeply respect the work of law enforcement agencies and pray for our officials daily, but as a pastor, I also felt deep concern for the man committing the crimes. The church is a place of refuge for any repentant sinner, regardless of the sins. I am also committed to law enforcement and appropriate retribution for offenses against society.

I shared the frustration of law officials at the lack of evidence and the pressures they felt from public criticism at the prolonged investigation of the crimes. But I do condemn their use of psychics and "spiritualist" mediums to find clues. That decision showed the extent of their frustration and their recognition that supernatural powers were somehow at work in the killer(s). However, their total miscomprehension of the dimensions of spiritual warfare involved in the crimes is evident. They called for help from those in alliance with demonic spirits to try to confront one under the control of those spirits.

The most recent encounter I have had with strong seductive spirits was in the Atlanta airport several weeks ago. I felt the power of oppressive spirits even before I recognized their source. I heard a crowd of people and turned around to see one of America's most famous rock stars as he passed me accompanied by his entourage. His concerts have filled the Omni in Atlanta numerous times with thousands of strongly impressionable young people who buy his records, tapes, and videos, and plaster his pictures on their bedroom walls or in their lockers at school.

As our eyes met, I saw the tortuous, demonic powers which magnetize his performances. He actually turned around as he walked by me, holding on to the confrontation of our spirits in those few, eternal seconds. I don't condemn him; I want him to be free. The heart of God is always moved with compassion toward those who are in bondage. Usually those who are powerfully used for evil also have tremendous potential to influence others for good once they are set free.

I wish I could say that the powers I saw in that young man are unusual, but I've confronted them repeatedly, especially in young people who have opened their spirits with drugs, occult activity or the aggressive pursuit of worldly trends as they try to "belong." Sometimes they are children from strong, Christian families who have tried desperately to reach them.

The Church needs to wake up and get into the battle against Satan's kingdom of sex. Now is the time to challenge worldly concepts of sexuality with alternatives that offer people a choice, a solution to the emptiness of constant self-gratification which never really satisfies. Only God's people can witness to His goodness in even the most intimate aspects of His intentions in creation.

Sex is God's idea. Christian sexuality is as much a demonstration of God's goodness and love as giving to the poor or sharing the plan of salvation with someone. Christian sexual intimacy is a witness to the world of love relationships which are given and blessed by God. The challenge to the worldly kingdom of sex by God's people is necessary to become that adequate witness which God requires in the earth before Christ returns. God is searching for people who are boldly challenging every worldly distortion of His goodness and love. The kingdoms of this world shall become the Kingdom of our God, and all things—every aspect of our lives— shall glorify Him as we walk daily in confidence, freedom and the power of the Holy Spirit.

2

A WHOLESOME CONCEPT
OF LOVE

One out of every two marriages ends in divorce. I have seen the devastation of many broken homes in my forty years of ministry. Many times divorce leads to emotional degradation, and sometimes even to physical or mental problems. Many times a divorce causes the lives of children to become very complicated.

The six-year-old daughter of one of our staff members asked her mother if she was planning to marry again. She told her mother, "Mom, you can't do that because it would complicate my life."

Children know how their parents' choices affect them. Sometimes it seems inevitable that divorces occur. We have many people who are in this situation, even in leadership in the Church. I do not condemn people. I war the evil that happens sometimes because people don't know how to prepare against complications in their lives.

Many people have been destroyed because they thought they were "in love" when they made lifelong commitments based on transient feelings. In the Greek language, the word "love" uses three words to connote three different kinds of affections.

The first Greek term for love is "eros." My definition of "eros" love would be, "love which is expressed physically." Eros has to do primarily with instinctive responses in affections. Eros is used in referring to an animalistic drive. The drive within an animal which causes him to mate is primarily the result of a powerful physical magnetism. Eros expresses itself differently in male and female. In the male, eros probably can be expressed without any moral responsibility whatsoever.

Physical love is more of an act to a male. I am not implying that men are like animals, I am simply saying that instinctive responses exist in people as well as in animals. We are basically no different from animals in this respect. A powerful magnetic force within us is animalistic in that we are attracted to the opposite sex out of instinct. Anybody who denies having that instinctive drive is lying because eros is a natural desire to mate. Eros is that desire in us to relate to another person in an intimate way. Without proper Christian control, eros is expressed many times in lust.

Not always, sometimes emotional damage, fatigue, insecurity, or illness can override the natural desire,

I react negatively to the phrase, "falling in love." I think "falling in love" is exactly what that expression implies. It is like falling into a trap. I do not think that Christians should ever "fall" in love. "Falling in love" indicates an uncontrollable passion that will put people together, sometimes for wrong purposes. Without understanding that innate drive, many of our young people are directed in relationships by their own feelings. Marriages established on feelings seldom last for very long. Feelings are non-directive. Marriage relationships based on feelings can be expressed in any emotional direction.

To most people, overpowering feelings of wanting someone may come as a surprise. A young man may be standing in a department store and a beautiful girl passes by him. He immediately feels attracted to her. A mature Christian man knows how to handle those feelings. But the man who has carnal thought processes does not know how to channel those feelings positively. He only suppresses his desires because he is afraid of the law, somebody punching him in the nose, or being rejected.

Many people are emotionally confused because they do not understand the purposes of God. They don't understand Kingdom motivations. I believe the Kingdom of God is a reality. Kingdom people do not live in some super-structured spirituality. When eros alone controls one's relationships, that person is frustrated by unsatisfied, unstable longings. Infatuation moves from one person to another. Infatuation may be with one person one week and the next week with someone else.

Eros is not a dependable criterion for mature love. Its strong sexual stimulation feeds the pornographic markets. Eros is depicted as the norm in relationships by the movie industry. Advertisers use sexual suggestions of eros to sell their products. Unfortunately, far too often, marriages begin with this kind of love. Too many serious commitments are motivated by little more than physical attractions. Young teens, thirteen and fourteen-year-olds, need to understand the dangers of these relationships. Most young people do not know the differences between mature and immature love. All they care about is how someone makes them feel or how a person looks. Relationships always fail when they are based on surface appearances and feelings.

Eros love primarily satisfies a person's needs. In other words, eros satisfies "number one." It has no desire to involve another person except by saying, "I want that pretty woman," or, "I want that handsome man," or, "I want that kind of sexual stimulation." Unfortunately, eros is where most love relationships begin and end. The one central issue is, "I want you, and I have a desire for you." Some individuals respond to eros relationships simply by feeling wanted. No matter what else is true concerning mature love, certain people must feel "needed" by someone. This desire is especially true in women. If some women feel needed, they are instantly in love. Marriages based on need alone usually do not survive. Some men, because of eros sexual desires, will suddenly "need" a physical relationship. A man might tell himself that he "needs to make love."

A characteristic of an eros relationship is that it changes with various partners. Affections can change almost instantaneously. The object of love can change with only a thought or fantasy. Sexual attraction can change in a matter of hours from one person to another. When uncontrolled and unrelated to a total comprehension of love, eros finally develops into lusts and uncontrolled passions.

Eros emphasizes concerns such as, "How do I look?" Eros focuses on the outward man. "How do I impress you?" "What should I wear?" "How do I compare with other women?" "How do I compare with other men?" Eros establishes credibility and self-esteem by comparison. "I am too short." "I am too fat." One of the fruits of eros love is vanity. Many times eros emotions are controlled by the spirit of vanity because a person feels that love comes only by projecting a desirable image. Eros is a vital part of the total concept of wholesome love created by God. But when an entire relationship is based on eros love, that relationship has little chance of survival. Probably the majority of love relationships are based on this criterion of love.

Eros emphasizes physical love, but man is body, soul and spirit. Because people do not understand themselves as three-part beings, they allow themselves to follow passions driven by uncontrolled desires and emotions. People who don't understand their emotional needs can even be drawn to people of the same sex. Eros feelings can stimulate bisexual and, in some cases, even homosexual activities. Eros arouses the source of our emotions which needs physical interaction with another person. Experiencing these feelings does not mean that people are atheistic or that they are going to hell. Eros desires are a normal part of real life.

Many people ask, "Did Jesus have these feelings?" I believe that He did. In a day when Jewish men were not supposed to have any public or social contact with women, the gospels clearly affirm that women followed Jesus. Women ministered to Him. When He visited in homes, women were a vital part of His interaction on that social level. His social interaction brought the accusation of His being a "wine-bibber and a glutton" (Luke 7:34). Jesus spent very little time addressing sins in personal or carnal areas. He focused His ministry on addressing the sins of the spirit which expose man's hypocrisy and pride. Jesus was strong against the Pharisees in their false righteousness, but He was gentle and compassionate to the vilest sinners who came to Him for help.

The Pharisees behaved as if normal human needs never existed. The Pharisees never admitted to having the kinds of normal feelings which I have just described. I can't imagine the explanation they gave for how they raised families. Jesus attacked their hypocrisy. He said, "The Kingdom of God is here! The Kingdom is consciousness and awareness. The Kingdom is life as God actually created it to be." Physical desires are an important part of man as God created him. Until we understand and acknowledge this area of man's nature, we will never be able to move to the higher spiritual dimensions that God has given us the capacity to enjoy. Paul said, "That which is natural is first, and the natural is followed by that which is spiritual" (I Corinthians 15:46). Paul asks, "Does not nature itself teach you certain things?" (I Corinthians 11:14). Our feelings will teach us if we listen to them. A wholesome concept of love allows us to lead our emotions rather than having emotions lead us. If eros rules a person's affections, relationships will always be shallow and unstable.

Another Greek word for love is "philia." I define this kind of love primarily with its basis on personal ideals and values. Philia love flows from the soul of man. This love is based on one's own inner-consciousness. Philia begins in relationships as a decision-making process. Unlike eros which is motivated by instinct, philia is motivated by a decision.

Philia is affection resulting from "soul mating." Two people are attracted to one another through common interests and mutual needs. A philia relationship becomes somewhat of an arrangement. Many marriages in Eastern countries and old European customs of parents arranging marriages for their children come from this understanding of love. Parents made arrangements with other parents in the best interests of their children. Their choices were based on similarities in family background and common interests. Parents would look at all the factors related to their children's backgrounds, education and goals and simply work out an arrangement with another family.

Today, philia motivates a woman living by herself to decide that she needs someone to take care of her. She doesn't make that decision because of any particular sexual or spiritual desires. In her soulish understanding of her needs, she simply makes a decision. She says, "I don't need to live alone for the rest of my life."

A man might say, "My little tootsies get cold at night, and I would like to have a warm body lying beside me." He makes a decision to find a wife so that he won't have to live alone any longer. Perhaps he remembers that God said, "It is not good for man to be alone." He makes that decision to marry, and immediately he begins to look for a wife who will be compatible with him. Perhaps he doesn't want to open cans any longer and he begins searching for a good cook.

Many relationships are built on this basis of love. Most marriages begin as a combination of eros and philia love. Even many Christians marry to satisfy physical desires and according to soulish decisions based on their interests. They say, "We think a lot alike." "We go to the same church." "We are both Christians." My years of experience in ministry assure me that this practical reasoning is not an adequate basis for marriage. Unfortunately, two Christians may be terrible partners in a marriage relationship. That fact is apparent to any pastor. The Church is no longer far behind the world in divorce statistics. Doesn't that say something to young Christians contemplating marriage? I'm sorry to say that most people refuse to listen to any advice on this subject until it is too late.

Sometimes parents stay together for the sake of their children. That agreement to maintain a family unit is an example of philia love. A husband and wife may have no more physical attraction for one another whatsoever, but they agree to stay together "until Jane grows up and leaves home." That agreement is not an adequate basis to maintain a good relationship, however. A businessman might reason to himself, "I am a professional executive. A divorce would hurt my chances to move up in the company. I can't afford a marital separation right now." A wife and mother might say to herself, "I don't want anybody to get hurt."

Philia affects the area having to do with personal decisions and one's conscious determinations based on circumstances. Philia love is only one step above responding to our needs as animals do. Animals move purely and simply by instincts, out of their sensual stimulations such as smell and appetite. All of us have those drives and until we recognize them, we will never be mature. We will never be able to experience and maintain a wholesome concept of love without understanding our motivations and God's intentions in creating us as we are.

Some people never associate the eros desires of their love life with any other emotions they may feel. For many of these people, sexual enjoyment occurs only in illegitimate affairs outside of a formally committed relationship. Sex must involve some sinful act to arouse the flesh. Many times people have strong sexual desires easily expressed before marriage and then become impotent after marriage because sex is no longer exciting. "It is the forbidden sweets that touch the flesh," the writer of Proverbs says (Proverbs 9:17). These people respond only to the allurement of sexual pleasure behind somebody's back. Everyone has in them a touch of that allurement to "the forbidden." Those who react to that charge by shaking their heads, "No, no, not me!" are usually the most guilty.

We all need to recognize and understand our desires and motives. We need to understand the feelings taking place inside us. In examining inner reality, we can then make good decisions on how to express our desires properly. We need to honestly ask ourselves, "What will be the result of this relationship? "What will be the end result of my conduct?"

Many times we have heard about some married man running away with his secretary or his next door neighbor. After being away from home for two or three weeks, he comes crawling back to the family he left behind. He has lost everything he really valued. He has lost relationships, security and self-respect. His life is in ruin because he moved out of instinct, thinking that he had finally discovered the way to go. Once he arrived at the end of that path, he thought, "God, have mercy! I didn't want this!" He became homesick for his kids and wanted to go back home to his precious wife, but the door was closed. A man or woman in that situation does not understand what has taken place inside. Their movements were directed by what they wanted and by certain kinds of distorted decision-making processes.

The third Greek term that defines love is "agape." Agape love has its source in God. The strength of agape love is its divine source. Because the source of agape is infinitely connected with universal laws, it is not transient or momentarily expressed. Agape is a basic quality of life flowing within us from God and flowing from us to others. Agape love involves the will of man. It involves the intentions of God within us, the Spirit of God intermingled with the spirit of man. Man is comprised of spirit, soul and flesh. Eros and philia can operate totally apart from divine intervention, but agape demands divine intervention and cannot operate apart from God's will. It demands prayer, spiritual authority and spiritual covering.

Agape in relationships motivates our charitable acts toward others. References to love (I Corinthians 13) say, "Though I speak with the tongues of men and of angels, and have not 'agape' (not eros or philia)." Agape love fulfills God's intentions because our good intentions alone profit nothing. Our efforts become only "sounding brass and tinkling cymbals." Jesus left us a new commandment: love [agape] one another. This agape is not contingent upon how we feel. Love becomes a commandment—a decision-making response by the Spirit.

Only agape applies when we talk about a couple as "those whom God hath joined together." God doesn't join two people together only by the flesh. He also supernaturally joins them together in the Spirit. A couple joined together on other levels are not really in essence "married" with a sacramental marriage or in that mysterious union which symbolizes Christ and His Church.

Even within churches today, I would estimate that seventy-five to ninety percent of people joined in wed-

39

ding ceremonies marry with philia or eros motivations instead of agape. The goal of agape love is to meet the needs of others. Eros love insists, "I want, I need!" In contrast, agape says, "God in me wants to meet your needs." When we understand agape love, it becomes the most satisfying possible response in affection because it far transcends eros. We cannot fake agape love. Agape love gives a person self-control over his (her) sexual desires. Agape love is the key to our becoming that channel for the Spirit to lead the flesh. When the flesh leads, it gratifies only itself.

In the forty years that I have counseled people, many of them have told me the frustrations of their sexual lives. Their frustrations are almost always because they live out their desires on eros and philia levels of love. A man who allows sexual thoughts to build up in his mind all day long comes home and acts like "a chicken on a June-bug." His poor little wife asks, "What was that?" How can that couple understand what it means to give themselves to one another? Their intimacy is controlled by frustrated mental processes. Their mental attitudes control their bodily responses. Two people controlled by the Holy Spirit have the ability to minister agape in physical intimacy. Without God, all a couple can do is to gratify themselves. When God is in us, our first motivation is to gratify someone else. A million miles separate these motives for "making love."

"God so loved the world that He gave" (John 3:16). God gave to the world because He loved the world. He "gave His only begotten Son" to satisfy the needs of the world. If a person doesn't have this kind of love and will honestly admit that, I recommend a delay in getting married. Relationships built upon the first two levels of love (eros and philia) will not survive with any kind of real satisfaction. The years change people's mental concepts and when marriages are not of the Spirit, those relationships have difficulty lasting.

Changing concepts during middle age cause some people to experience what is called "the forty-year-old blues." Men also go though "menopause" or a mid-life crisis. As a matter of fact, men probably live in menopause all their lives. They are naturally grumpy. Men are created for headship and when that role becomes frustrated, they don't know what to do with their bottled-up energy. Men were created to go out and seek provision for their households. They instinctively want to be hunters. Because we don't recognize or require that expression in our society, men suffer a lot of frustration.

Agape love produces life in another. Agape is that "quickening" force that Paul describes. Because Christ dwells in us, we are "quickened" by His resurrection power (Romans 8:11). I believe agape love quickens life in others around us and especially in our companions. Agape quickens life in all our relationships.

Many times, the partner whom we think is guilty in a relationship problem is not the one who started that problem at all. Perhaps a sanctimonious woman did not know how to relate to a total concept of love. Perhaps she did not know that eros is an absolutely necessary, healthy part of a man's needs. When those needs

41

were expressed, she rejected him and called him "a dog." If she had understood his expressions of love and lifted them to a higher dimension with tenderness, that need in him could have been expressed in a proper, godly way.

When a woman comes to me crying because her honeymoon is over and she thinks her husband is already looking over his shoulder at somebody else, I calmly say to her, "Maybe you are not being the total type of woman that he needs. Sometimes he needs a mother, and in a subtle way you need 'to mother' him. At times he needs a faithful and virtuous companion, and other times (though you may not like what I am going to say), he wants a sexy woman."

Some react by saying, "A Christian woman cannot be that!" A mature, Christian woman is not stupid. She needs to use her femininity in the proper framework to excite her husband. I am convinced that most of the time the trouble with impotent men is stupid women. But many women do not release their sexual aggressions because they are afraid of their husbands' jealousy. Once a wife expresses her capacity for passion and her husband experiences it, he is afraid to let her out of his sight. He sometimes becomes very possessive, and the first killing blow to a passionate woman is a possessive husband. Mature love is being able to turn someone loose knowing that person will always come back. That is mature love.

Agape love gives one the ability to think as God thinks. In the Garden of Eden, God allowed us the choice of obeying or disobeying Him. He turned us loose. He said, "I put a choice out there for you. You have freedom to choose 'the tree of life' or 'the tree of the knowledge of good and evil' or total obedience. Now, go." Agape love in parents releases their children when the proper time comes. Many people never know how to release their children. Unfortunately, some parents release their children too quickly. Agape love is the mind of Christ in us. The Holy Spirit lets us know when to turn loose, simply back off, move in, extend loving arms, refuse to give any support at all, patronize them, and also look them in the eyes and say, "We are not going to agree to that."

Agape love produces life. It releases the best desires for a companion. If men and women could release their own desires before they reached such points of irreconcilable difficulties, counselors could help save many relationships. Once someone walks into an office and says, "I am going to get a divorce," they have given an ultimatum. How can that counselor possibly be effective at that point? Instead, when problems begin to surface, a husband or wife should walk into a Spirit-filled counselor's office and say, "My marriage needs help. I submit myself."

Counseling is useless if a person refuses to submit himself to a counselor's advice. No one needs to go to a surgeon if he is not going to listen to the doctor's recommendations. Most people have already made up their minds about what they will do before they ever walk into a pastor's office. I can tell nine times out of ten, in about ten minutes of conversation, whether I am going to be able to help an individual or not. Most people come to a pastor "for counseling" simply hoping that they will get confirmation on the plans they've already made. It won't work that way! The ability to receive counseling means a personal resignation by saying, "I have been wrong. I know I have made mistakes. My marriage is falling apart. Now, tell me what to do."

Until a couple learns to trust the leadership of their church, they can never receive help from them. Jesus could not work miracles in Nazareth because of the unbelief of people who knew Him only as the carpenter's son. They did not believe in God's power at work in Him. In order for people to receive the kind of ministry they need to receive, agape love is absolutely necessary. God will not go around the channel or direction of His resources. God has neither para-ministries nor appendage ministries. Rebellious ministries do exist, but they are like cancer cells to the Church. They cut off God's lifeline and resources because people are not in God's appointed structure to receive His help.

I believe if the structure in God's house were set in order, we could defeat Satan's attacks to break up Christian families today. Families need to trust spiritual leadership to discern a situation and say, "That is your flesh," or "That is your 'soulish man' causing this problem," or "The problem is a void in understanding the spiritual aspects of this situation and relying on the resources that God gives to us." God's Word and understanding God's provisions in His Church must be taken seriously if marriages are going to be saved.

Agape love is the kind of love that the Apostle Paul

refers to when he says, "For those who live according to the flesh set their minds on the things of the flesh, but those who live according to the Spirit, the things of the Spirit" (Romans 8:5). When we are led by the Holy Spirit, the flesh is under control. When both the animal nature within us and the soulish, intellectual man which makes our decisions are under the direction of the Holy Spirit, we will make decisions according to God's divine intentions. In order to enter into this dimension of thinking, feeling and living, the baptism of the Holy Spirit is necessary.

For two people to achieve oneness in the right kind of love relationship, both people must be baptized in the Holy Spirit. When the Holy Spirit controls the lives of two people who are in love, eros and philia assume their rightful places in the relationship. The couple can express their instinctive, emotional desires, and they can also control them in a godly manner. They know how to be fulfilled in every aspect of love but always under the unction of the Holy Spirit. Many people say that having sex is incompatible with prayer and praising God. Those people are one hundred percent wrong. Expressions of love include a place for fulfilling physical desires under proper control as well as intimacy relating its source to God.

People experience healing in agape spiritual relationships. Many people can even be healed of physical sicknesses during sexual intimacy if that couple are Spirit-filled. Perhaps few pastors have ever taught that intimacy brings healing, but I contend this teaching to be a fact. Marriages based on agape relationships are such a refuge to those partners that agape love is also a primary source of healing. Nothing gives someone more acceptance or rejection than sexual love. Paul admonished us, "Present your bodies as a living sacrifice" (Romans 12:1). Our bodies become temples of the Holy Spirit.

Paul said in Romans that he loved Israel so much that he would count himself "accursed for their sakes" (Romans 9:3). That is a strong statement. He would agree to spending his life in hell if he could have saved them. Some women won't even give their bodies to erring husbands to save them. Some men get so fixed in their own possessiveness that they close themselves away or go lie on a couch to punish their wives. Men who don't give their wives the kind of love that a spiritual man can give eventually wonder why their wives don't respect them. A Spirit-filled man transcends a woman's emotional problems to such a degree that he becomes a life-giving source to her in an intimate relationship. Sex is a God-given resource. Agape sexual love is a spiritual experience which has the power to overcome physical problems.

God is male and female. In a marriage relationship, God blesses a man and a woman who honor Him. Many people who are in lifestyles opposed to God must enter a godly lifestyle with the right kind of spiritual relationships in order to receive physical healing. The level of our love affects the soul, and our thought processes affect the body.

God is calling Christian men and women to expand their concepts of love. We must honestly admit the eros of our desires and the philia of our reasoning as we share the agape of God's love in us with others. The world is waiting for examples of a "better way" to live and love. Only God's people possess the revolutionary possibility of becoming that Kingdom prototype which will say, "We have the solutions. We are a demonstration of the creation of man—male and female—as God intended us to be."

3

SEXUAL HONESTY

Jesus is unchangeable and His Kingdom is unshakable. Unlike His Kingdom, life on earth within the existing social structure is highly volatile. Commonly accepted social morality changes rapidly. Modern morality has shifted drastically from the almost prudish code of the Victorian era to the extreme "free love" morality of recent years. Increasing acceptance of sexual perversion is rampant in Western society. Morality changes, but the basic needs of people don't change with the times or the culture. Social philosophy and the expressions of that philosophy may change, but the principles of true fulfillment and joy in relationships are timeless.

The Holy Spirit is the same today as He has always been. The power of the Holy Spirit did not diminish when the apostles who surrounded Jesus died. No particular virtues are ascribed to the prophets of the Old or New Testament. They were prophets. The Bible said that the Word of God came to us by the inspiration of the Holy Spirit as He moved upon holy men of old.

The prophets of the Old Testament were not only men, some were also rather carnal men in their personal lives. They were men who were on the spiritual mountaintop one day and in the valley the next day. Elijah is a classic example of that spiritual diversity. The Lord used some of His prophets to do very strange things. One walked around nude and another married a harlot. Prophets are a strange breed. God develops their uniqueness so that He can speak many times in peculiar circumstances and situations.

As I enter into the discussion of some very personal areas of life, I will say nothing that I do not believe is designated of the Holy Spirit. However, this discussion has two distinct levels. Some statements are given by command and some are given by permission of the Lord. Statements given by command, I always attribute to the Holy Spirit. Other statements are spoken by God's permission. I attribute those beliefs to my spiritual understanding and experiences based on many years of ministry and fellowship with God.

In my own spirit, I have permission to say some things that might not be given by direct command of the Holy Spirit. I will make a distinction as we progress in this study. Remember those two levels of discussion always exist. "Thus saith the Lord" is always spoken by command. "In my opinion, this is what the Holy Spirit is saying" means that I am speaking by permission. A difference in obedience is required between a command of the Holy Spirit and words spoken to the Church by permission. Most of this teaching is spoken by permission. When we understand that principle, these preliminary statements become very important.

Some issues are so close to us that we don't like to deal with them. We become somewhat uncomfortable discussing certain topics. In I Corinthians 7, Paul addressed some critical issues that he faced as an apostle to the Church. Paul dealt with a problem in his day of Christians' believing that Jesus Christ was coming back immediately to establish the Kingdom. They thought that Jesus Christ had gone into the heavens for a very short period of time and would come back quickly. Paul was not addressing an issue we have today, but the same principles apply.

Now concerning the things of which you wrote to me: It is good for a man not to touch a woman. Nevertheless, because of sexual immorality, let each man have his own wife, and let each woman have her own husband. Let the husband render to his wife the affection due her, and likewise also the wife to her husband. The wife does not have authority over her body, but the husband does. And likewise the husband does not have authority over his own body, but the wife does. Do not deprive one another except with consent for a time, that you may give yourselves to fasting and prayer; and come together again so that Satan does not tempt you because of your lack of self-control. But I say this as a concession, not as a commandment . . . Now to the married I command, yet not I but the Lord: A wife is not to depart from her husband. (I Corinthians 7:1-6, 10)

If we take this passage to apply to every generation and problem in marriages, how would we harmonize this scripture with the one that says, "When a man finds a wife, he finds a good thing"? This passage in Corinthians says that it is good for a man not to touch a woman. What did Paul mean? Should a man marry a woman and never touch her? No. Paul was dealing with a specific issue in a local church as an apostle, and God gave him authority to make those judgments. God said that if we don't learn to judge ourselves, we are no better than the world. Paul gave a very practical solution to the problem in that church when he said, "Nevertheless, because of sexual immorality, let each man have his own wife, and let each woman have her own husband." Paul is almost saying to that church, "Don't get married unless you cannot control your passions. If you just cannot exert self-control, get married."

Paul probably held that opinion, but that does not mean Paul's opinion expressed in this passage applies in the twentieth century. Another revelation says, "In the last days, they will forbid eating meat and marrying" (I Timothy 4:3). Understand that God must address specific situations in every generation. He must deal with specific needs. Principles do not vary, but God's permission to address specific situations will vary from generation to generation. We must understand Paul's thinking.

I will shock some people when I write that I do not believe Paul totally understood marriage from a personal perspective. If Paul had been married, he had probably known a very disappointing marriage. I may possibly shake some immature Christians who are not going to understand this opinion, but Paul is not a good marriage counselor to every generation. If indeed Paul had been married, he was either a widower or his own marriage had fallen apart. Paul did not necessarily have the knowledge to speak out of his own experiences on the subject of marriage. He talked about "due benevolence." The worst thing a woman could say to her husband is, "I am going to give you 'due benevolence.' " The worst thing a husband could say to his wife is, "My back is hurting and I am tired, but I am still going to give you 'due benevolence.' "

Paul was not setting forth a God-given revelation on relationships. He was dealing with specific problems in a specific church. He goes on to say that a wife does not have rights over her own body, but her husband does. In other words, bringing a wife to satisfaction in a sexual relationship is left to her husband. Paul goes on to say that likewise the husband does not have rights over his own body, but his wife does. The wife has power to bring satisfaction to her husband. Paul's mentality is that the only reason to be married and enjoy a sexual relationship is to keep a person from getting into fleshly sins. I say without any apology, I do not believe that. I don't believe that is the total purpose of marriage. That same reasoning does not concur with Paul's revelation in Ephesians 5 when he was speaking under commandment.

In Ephesians 5 Paul said that marriage relationships should be compared to Christ and His Church. When Jesus dealt with the obedience of His disciples, He said to them, "Love Me and be My disciples." He did not call them to "due benevolence" or to a sense of duty. Tithing and service to God is a dimension of love. We soar in the Spirit and give to God as He prospers us. What Paul is saying in I Corinthians 7 is not God's perfect commandment. In verse 6, Paul makes that point clear by his own admission. Paul did not have a revelation about marriage, he had an opinion. If Paul had received a revelation on marriage, his words would be absolutely unchangeable. He would say, "Thus saith the Lord." Most of Paul's writings are direct commandments of God, but some passages very carefully imply, "I speak here with my opinion as an apostle and as my thinking relates to your local situation."

Unfortunately, many people take certain passages and build entire strategies of counseling in relationships on scriptures in which Paul was writing by permission. I want to share some insights by commandment of the Holy Spirit that I believe differ from Paul's. "Now to the married I command, yet not I but the Lord: A wife is not to depart from her husband" (verse 10). Paul emphasized that this is not just his opinion. Verse ten is a "Thus saith the Lord," indicating that Paul's teaching on marriage is also written in two dimensions.

After forty years of being called of God and moving through various phases of ministry, I will assume the right to speak as no young pastor or young prophet may speak. I do not apologize for saying that I speak both by permission and by authority to reveal the heart of God.

I am going to share portions of a letter. The content of this letter is strong language for some people. Those offended by "sexual" words should not read any further. This is a letter that a woman wrote to her husband after the couple had encountered difficulties in their marriage and were engaged in pastoral counseling. In this letter, the wife begins to make herself very vulnerable:

". . . There are two key issues on my heart besides the one I have already discussed. One is my low self-image and the other is our sex life. I will probably address them interchangeably. I believe it is time to be serious about this work and to do the will of the heavenly Father. To grow any further than we have, the following issues must be resolved once and for all. The Holy Spirit has spoken this to me through pastoral counseling. Either I finally get past all this, or I will be in serious trouble. I have promised you nothing but the truth, so today will be the beginning of that promise.

"It is strange to me, Sweetheart, that we always try to hide, pretend or cover-up the issues that we really want to address most. I want to go back and help you understand the areas I have come to understand."

This woman had experienced an abortion early in her life.

"The morning after the abortion, something in me died. However, that is not the main issue. Prior to the abortion, because of my needs stimulated by a perverted spirit that ruled me and my family, I chose to run with a wild crowd with shallow values. There was one boy with whom I would sneak out at night, and we would go to his basement or off in his car somewhere. One night he took photographs of me, or at least I thought he did. He subsequently blackmailed me for other favors. He did rape me finally. Otherwise, we were only fooling around. After the rape, I broke up with him for good. Thank God, he got drafted.

"I was always reaching out and looking for something. From my earliest memories I was called 'the black sheep of the family,' 'the late bloomer,' one who was talented like my older brother

and sister, but without enough intelligence to learn to play an instrument. I never had enough motivation to learn to read or spell, much less to play an instrument.

"My instrument was the stereo. Music and movies were big attractions in my life. My heroes were actors and actresses. I would spend hours and hours alone with these celebrity characters in my imagination. I played their records and imitated their sounds. I would learn every word of their songs. I would pretend I was performing.

"Meanwhile, I ate for comfort and had only a very few friends. I was very lonely, poor and a lousy student. I set my life's goal on becoming a mother. I was deceitful and cunning and loved to be naughty because I simply could not do good things. This rebellion was not caused by a deliberate desire to be 'bad' or the result of silly feelings, but that was who I really was. I also had a deep compassion for people. My openness to others led me to friends who were all acne-faced, awkward, unsophisticated and shy. I felt sorry for them.

"Then I met you and you were my 'ace in the hole.' As you remember, I seduced you from the first time we were together. I knew sex was my only key because if I depended on my face, figure or brains, I was in trouble."

The issues most people talk about in their relationships are not their basic problems. A husband may scream at his wife because she did not have dinner prepared when his actual problem was that she would not love him the night before. A wife may scream at her husband because he does not take out the garbage or tend to the yard, when down inside she does not believe that he is romantically involved in their relationship anymore. We fail to get at the real issues. The honesty of this letter begins to uncover the real issues.

After an abortion, something happens to many women which they are never quite able to identify. That was true in this case. This quick and easy "solution" to an unwanted pregnancy often brings with it long-term guilt and sexual anxiety.

How many teenagers (for reasons that they don't even understand) choose to run with wild crowds? Perhaps they have poor relationships with their fathers. Perhaps they are frustrated about relationships and think that experimenting sexually will solve their problems.

In her letter, this woman said that her "instrument" became the stereo. Some kids become so dependent on music and their stereos that they don't even know it has become their expression. Music becomes a hiding place and refuge for them. Sometimes loud music takes them away from other realities. They become addicted to volume without even understanding the reasons.

Movies became a focus in her life. She would pretend she was the actress. She did not like her own world, therefore she became addicted to imagination and pretense. She had never identified who she really was. Her low self-esteem caused her not to want to be herself. She tried to be someone else.

Sex has two stimulations. One motivation is evil and sinful and carnalities turn it on. The other motivation is godly love in a relationship free to enjoy total expression of love. Most people live in a mixture of these two. Some people enjoy sex before they get married and yet become totally impotent after marriage when sex is acceptable. These same people could cheat on a husband or wife, and sex would once again be very enjoyable. Until we address issues like these, we don't really know the proper motivation for love. Pornographic materials would be totally unnecessary if everyone were in God-given relationships.

The kinds of people we feel drawn toward is a reliable indication of who we are. If we are always drawn to people who are underlings or defeated "down-and-outers," sometimes the attraction is not because God in us loves them. They may relate to our own self-identity. We need to know why we feel certain ways. Why would a person be drawn to "white trash"? Why would a white person always be drawn to a black person who may be from another station in life? Why would someone be drawn to an indigent? If someone reaches a place of economic success, why must he then give money back to people who are trapped because of their race or circumstances? Until we address our motives, we don't know who we are or why we do the things we do.

The woman writing the letter tried to seduce her husband the first time she met him. Sex was the only tool she felt she had to make her attractive to him. None of her perceptions were really true. Her problem was her own image of herself. She could easily have been a most attractive woman. A few years ago, one of the most beautiful little girls I had ever seen in my whole life told me that she thought she was ugly. I asked her why. She said that her father had treated her badly because she was ugly. She honestly did not know that she was an exceptional beauty. Beauty is not something definable. Beauty is in the eyes of the beholder.

I do know the young woman who wrote the letter, and she is a very beautiful and attractive woman. The point is that these are issues we don't deal with honestly because we don't understand the source of our feelings. Some people who believe that they are sexy and suave are definitely not. They go around swinging their hips, looking like they have a spider in their pants. They certainly are not sexy.

The way a person dresses and makes up himself (herself) is an indication of how much he(she) lacks self-esteem. If a dear, close friend were to come to someone's house and find the lady of the house in hair rollers, without make-up, and that woman runs screaming and yelling to try to fix herself up, she has a problem. Men and women must be careful not to depend on make-up and clothes instead of themselves. We can add all the pads in all the right places and still be absolutely insecure. We must learn to accept ourselves for who we are and find the image God has for us. Otherwise, we will always maintain a low self-image. A low self-image can create a world of problems.

"I was in trouble. The only thing I had to offer you was sex. I can remember being amazed at your parents' wealth. As it turns out, they really might not have been that wealthy, but by comparison, they were definitely a cut above my family. I remember thinking that you were rich, cute and smart. You could be my ticket out of all my negative feelings. You would make me somebody, and I'd even have money, too. You know the rest.

"You don't know the sick feelings I get in the pit of my stomach when the subject of sex comes up. I have had a difficult time thinking of sex as either fun or relaxing. I cannot bear to begin

any kind of sexual gymnastics. I see you in my mind as only wanting to use me to achieve your own self-centered desires. Sex does not make me feel pretty or sexy. I do not have an attractive body. I do not feel that I give anything to you other than a place to relieve your own physical pressures. Fooling around is very distasteful to me, probably because of my past.

"Motherhood. What a word! God, I love those children. I feel so inadequate to teach them how they should really feel about life. I know it all in my mind, but I beg God not to let me hurt them. Praise God, I have finally dealt with my temper (like my dad's temper that was so violent). I do feel free of that spirit now. I can remember so clearly the fear I had of my dad. I can remember the way he would come back to me after he had abused me. He would try to hold me and tell me that he loved me. I would cringe and feel sick inside. I had such hate for myself then because I could not be whatever he wanted. I do not want to go on with this . . .

"I have never wanted anyone's pity for me. I begged God that if He gave me a little girl, He would give her your 'skinny' genes. I want her to be your princess so badly. I want for you to take her in your arms and make her feel like she is a real princess. With such pride and pleasure, teach her that she is beautiful. Let her know that in your heart she can do no wrong. Make her a princess. I want her to grow up and feel secure about knowing that you are her daddy and you always will be."

People make a terrible mistake when they marry to get out of problems. Marriage is not the solution to anyone's problems. Marriage means a covenant between two people whom God has designated to demonstrate an intimacy which reflects Christ's relationship with the Church. How many marriages begin with an escape mentality? People want to get out of trouble or to become what others think they should be. One of the worst fears motivating marriage is the fear of being an "old maid." Fear of getting married should be so strong in Christians that marriage occurs only as a response to the leading of the Holy Spirit. Making ourselves totally vulnerable to another human being calls for a very great emotional maturity.

Now, many years later, every time the subject of sex comes up, she feels sick to her stomach. Her husband probably doesn't understand her feelings. He thinks, "Why doesn't she respond to me?" She is still responding to thought patterns that involved her in sexual activity before marriage. Many girls involve themselves in sexual relationships in high school for approval and position. Often they never understand the purpose of sex. They spend the rest of their lives using sex as a way to accomplish certain goals. The woman writing the letter couldn't relax during sex with her husband because it was work. Sex had been her way out of unhappy circumstances.

Romance which is used to keep a husband at home is wrong. If affection is used to keep a wife from running around, the motive is wrong. Sex has two God-given purposes. The first is to create babies and replenish the world. The second purpose is to establish an intimate relationship in which two human beings interact under God in a way that pleases the Lord. To use sex as a tool, weapon, punishment or enticement is sinful, immoral and evil. Most people begin sexual relationships for the wrong reasons.

By permission of the Holy Spirit, I am going to address some misunderstandings of men and women. Couples who fight so they can make up are not only carnal, they are immoral. A seductive spirit rules that relationship. The tougher or more violent that spirit becomes, the more response it will draw when making up. How wrong that is!

Parents who correct a child properly will speak love in their correction. Parents who cuddle and love their children because they feel guilty about the punishment they gave them totally destroy whatever correction was accomplished. A woman misses the purposes of intimacy when she knows she is wrong about something and tries to make it up to her husband in bed. A man who has treated his wife unfairly and tries to make it up to her by patting her on her fanny will not regain her trust. No wonder she expresses a negative reaction at his touching her. No wonder some women regard sex as if they were victims. They want more than someone who is kind and considerate only for sexual gratification. Too many people go from one extreme to another in their affections. In those extremes, a partner is always totally turned off and unable to respond physically. To try to force sexual response is abusive.

She felt regretful that her little girl had her genes. She prayed, "Don't let her be like me." Her prayer should have been, "God, I want her to be like me." A parent who has a sense of self-worth desires similarity in his(her) children. That is really a secret human desire—to reproduce ourselves in our children. We need to be able to admit that. Because she was not accepted, she felt her little girl would not be accepted for the same reasons.

She desires the security she never felt from her own father for her daughter. The worst mistake a dad can make is when he fails to make his daughter feel like she is a princess. The worst mistake a mother can make is to destroy the God-given self-image of her children. I would rather my daughters call me to pray for them than anybody else in the world. I would rather have them want me to touch, love and hold them than anybody else. If I have lived out God's love before them, I make them feel as if they are somebody important and have an important place in my life.

I don't apologize for using my children in my ministry. Many preachers' children become frustrated. They go into the world and seek things that never give satisfaction because their parents made them perform as perfect examples. They grow up feeling deprived of opportunities to learn and grow. If children have been in a family who always speak in public places, public speaking should be natural for them.

My brother Don and I have never known what it is to sit in a congregation. My dad was the pastor of a large Pentecostal church, and I sat on the pulpit with him from the time I was only a little boy. When I was twelve years old, I was the junior pastor of children's church. By the time I was fifteen years old, I was teaching a women's Bible class to women old enough to be my grandmothers. When I was seventeen, God called me to preach. At nineteen, I was a pastor. Why shouldn't I have been prepared?

God's will is not accidental. He knows what He is doing. The great Apostle Paul was taught at the feet of Gamaliel. God makes no mistakes in His choices. Family background is not always an indication of calling, but it certainly can be a great advantage in preparation. Don't apologize when this happens.

"I get so tired of trying to prove my self-worth. I finally realized my value did not come from being your 'Mrs.,' or from being a mother, or from being involved in a high-powered ministry. My identity doesn't come from having a college degree. My self-worth simply comes from belonging to Christ. That realization made me nervous because it is so simple. My worth is only in Him.

"I am tired of not being excited about sex. As you know, I have had my moments. I am sorry that you don't feel that you 'turn me on.' Frankly, you have done better than anybody else. It is probably worth mentioning that I never had a climax from the encounters in my adulterous fling. The situation was always so scary and guilt-producing that I never really got anything out of it. The pastor helped me to see that the supposed 'turn on' that I would get was the excitement of sin and not sex. I am sad to say that I do not know what to tell you to do to 'turn me on.' I know that I believe fully in my own inability for satisfaction and I don't blame you.

"You have a nice body. I think you have become very handsome after all these years, but I do get turned off by your manners. I don't know if these are normal irritations, but I'm bothered when you talk with food in your mouth. You often interrupt people when they speak. You seem to be always more interested in what you have to say than what others have to say. I feel it is very rude for you to fall asleep on people, particularly when we have guests, or when we are in God's house. I resent your wanting to make love when your face has a rough day-old beard.

"I do not really understand why I view sex as such a chore. I do not know whether sex is one of the ways I can show you that I love you. Sex is for you. You enjoy it. My only enjoyment is

because you enjoy it.''

Knowing who you are in Christ sounds so simple, and yet it gives a person self-worth as nothing else can. The answer to a positive identity is not college, job training, or finishing schools. Knowing who you are in Jesus Christ is the answer.

Sex was always so scary and guilt-producing that she never got anything out of it. Some say that fear of sex has not been true with them. They say, "Man, it was a whammo, whammo!" After they get married, the guilt will be such that if they had tremendous satisfaction before marriage, they will never be satisfied sexually unless they return to the original, sinful provocations. They will always need to be "turned on" by some fleshly thought. Unless they let God deal with flesh sins, their satisfaction is an aberration.

If, however, a girl always felt guilty and sexual experimentation for her was not a good experience before marriage, thank God because she still has a chance. When the real thing comes along, people know it. God-given oneness does not happen in the back seat of a car, beside the road somewhere, or in some cheap motel. If we could only know the real thing, what heartache and sorrow we could spare.

Many divorces begin with irritations caused by poor manners. Someone says, "What does talking with your mouth full have to do with sex?" Everything! Manners produce an image. Image-making is real. Uncouth, improper or unmannerly behavior is a misuse of someone else. Even by our words, we build an image in a wife's or husband's mind that reflects the person we are inside.

If a woman is constantly tearing down every pretty girl in sight, her husband may not tell her, but he knows she is insecure. A man may tear down every other man who has a strong body saying, "Have you noticed he has crooked teeth? But have you noticed, one of his ears is lower than the other?" All he is saying is that he doesn't trust his own self-image. We create an image no matter where we are.

Many men will laugh at the reference to a "day-old beard." Whether we know it or not, a beard does not feel particularly good to a woman. If a man grows a mustache or beard (which is all right; I am not warring that!), he should get permission from his wife. She has the right to say "no." During physical contact, a beard can become very uncomfortable. Many men say that they want to be "macho." They had better want to please their wives. Remember, a wife's interest in intimacy is more important than looks.

A person may think that little things are unimportant to his(her) lover, but consideration is essential to a good sexual relationship. A man should shave before making love to his wife if that helps her to know that her comfort is important to him. If a man shaves to go out in public, how much more should he be attentive to his wife by making her comfortable? These basic, little things make a big difference in the happiness of a marriage.

People say, "Well, if she doesn't want sex, she just doesn't want it." She wants it. She just doesn't want to be close to someone who is inconsiderate of her. He is not fulfilling her needs because he is not giving her an image that will make her respond. Some relationships are so mature and fulfilling that these little things would be incidental. But if a relationship has any rough edges, little things become critical. Please understand these principles. In many solidly knit relationships, these issues would be inconsequential, but where there is already tension in a relationship, little offenses can cause great irritation. If some husbands started to shave before going to bed, their wives would say, "Forget about it! For goodness sake, come on! Just forget about that!" But always remember that privately in the heart, sometimes thoughts are going on that we may not suspect.

Many people would say that they enjoy sex only because their partners do. If single gratification is the reason for intimacy, that unfulfilled partner has a problem. A woman destroys the manhood in a man by telling him that she is only his convenience. No one is really the convenience of someone else. Until two people can be involved in such a way that they interact in mutual joy and fulfillment, I promise that somewhere down the road, that relationship will sour.

I am going to make a statement that I believe God gives me permission to make. Some may not understand this conclusion, but just trust me as a man of God. A time will come when medical science will prove that many physical problems occur in women because they have not responded properly to sex. The natural God-given abilities to make love never functioned properly. Sexual gratification remained in a mentally and physically irritated state until after awhile, the body could no longer function properly.

Many women have hysterectomies early in life

because they are in unfulfilling sexual relationships.
The proper order in physical relationships is to let
nature dictate physical responses. Give nature enough
time to resolve tensions. Many young women I have
talked to across the years in earnest counseling sessions only needed time and reassurance to resolve
physical marital responses.

If a woman thinks her husband should come into the
bedroom, light a candle and kiss her toenails while he
strokes every single hair on top of her head, I suggest
she is an extremist. Between extremes is a proper way
and time to express love. If a person is physically too
tired to be responsive, he(she) should be honest and
say, "Honey, I really think we need to go to sleep
tonight." But if a partner makes excuses two, three, six,
seven or eight times in a row, he(she) is using physical
exhaustion to avoid intimacy. Honesty in the marriage
relationship is tremendously important.

Appropriate consideration is when one says, "Honey,
does this hurt you?" A woman appropriately says, "Let
me help you." If a husband is impotent, the reasons are
usually not his fault. Possibly his wife has given him
nothing to which he can respond. Usually impotence is
a problem in one's mind, not in the body. Impotence
can be caused by pressures or stress, but the solution
always involves both partners. Sexual problems for
one partner almost always require counseling with
both husband and wife.

*"I like the feeling of an orgasm and I do not mind working for
it. An added dimension in our lives now is the time pressures
—just being tired and mentally preoccupied. I simply do not need*

sex as much as you do. I don't prefer for you to show me your love in this manner. Dates, attention, flowers, cards, loving me when I am sick, understanding me when I am tired, giving me freedom to be myself, and family ties draw me closer to you.

"I honestly do not know what would draw me to you sexually. I believe that my losing weight and being sexy would only frustrate both of us. Yet, something inside of me longs to be a smaller size and to be able to buy pretty clothes easily. Something tells me that if I were thin, all the negative feelings I have about myself would change.

"After the abortion, I grew to resent sex even more. I didn't resent you, but just the 'physicalness' of sex itself. It became a tool for me to achieve some goal, satisfy you and get me pregnant.

"I am still angry with you for not giving me my engagement ring while we were dancing and sharing a lovely dinner. Instead, you took me to your dorm room. We had sex and then afterwards, flat on my back, you gave me my ring. I was sick, not to mention bitter and disappointed. I decided right then that no such thing as a princess existed. It is useless to try to believe she could exist. I suppose that is the reason I wanted a second ring so badly. Then there was the shameful, painful rushing of the wedding and bitter experiences following. Princesses didn't exist. What difference did the wedding make? The most beautiful time in our marriage was the birth of our first child.

"Your parents have never really accepted me. Both of us knew I was not good enough for you in the first place. I was just hurt that they confirmed my unworthiness all the time. It is no surprise that I have been an adulterous wife to you. I have been that to you from the very beginning."

Need levels vary. However, when two people become

one, needs will not vary with the couple. I am going to repeat that statement. If two are really one, need levels will not vary. During periods of pregnancy, or discomfort during menstruation, a husband will have no more need for sex than his wife does. Someone says, "Oh, man, I want sex like I want coffee—every morning." Well, that person needs to go live at the zoo!

Most men do not understand that romance is found in dates, attention, flowers, cards, loving her when she is sick, understanding her when she is tired, giving her freedom to be herself and family ties. If he thinks a woman changes after he marries her, he is totally wrong. He still needs to surprise her with M&M's and roses.

Losing weight will not change a woman's self-image. Certain bodily excesses are inappropriate and even uncomfortable when making love (or sometimes may even make it impossible), but weight is not the issue. If a woman is so interested in becoming thin that she loses her sexual desires, attractiveness has become counterproductive. Victims of anorexia have absolutely no sexual desires. Most of the time even their menstrual cycles cease. Some people become overweight to the extent that they become impotent or lose interest in sex. Isn't it wonderful to learn balance?

A woman's figure is not the main feature that attracts her husband. A nice body is an attractive addition, but a man falls in love with the spirit of a woman. I am going to say this to men, too: going to the spa and working for biceps so big that a man cannot put on a shirt will not make a woman love him. As a matter of fact, he can overdo exercise to such a degree that it will affect his potency. Learn that a nice body is not the key to sexual attraction. Love, kindness, acceptance, being there in life's storms and understanding the pressures of life make a person sexually attractive.

An abuse of alcohol not only does not make a person sexy, it makes them impotent. A man may think that his potency is just exaggerated and lifted to a higher level by alcohol, but sexual activity is as much a matter of the mind as of the body. Girls who drink two or three beers before they have sex have only killed their moral minds to such a degree that they can participate without guilt at that moment. We must learn these things before we waste our lives away.

It is not immoral to move forward in a relationship where the parents don't accept their child's choice of a mate, but that couple must adjust and predetermine how they are going to deal with the rejection. If they don't deal with parental rejection, I promise that the conflict will eventually affect the relationship.

When she (the writer of the letter) got married, she did not change from being an adulteress. Many people who have premarital sex, or sex out of a God-given relationship in unity of the Holy Spirit, never lose that adulterous spirit. Because it was not of God in the beginning, standing before a preacher or judge and saying words does not change God's will.

The letter concludes:

"Princesses do not exist. I love you. I need you. I believe in our marriage with great hope in my heart for what God will do. I want to be 'your' princess."

When I first read this letter, I wept because I saw so much reality in it. This letter said so many things I

71

have dealt with for so many years. I thought, "God, I will not allow this opportunity to go by without making some comments by permission of the Holy Spirit to address problems which exist throughout the Church."

Her husband did not make her feel like a princess. Princesses exist because someone makes a woman feel like she is a princess. Some husbands would like to make their wives into a princess, but the wife will not become one because of her own inability to discipline herself. She can never accept the mantle of being a princess. Many women, however, would be princesses if their husbands made them so.

But let me turn the coin quickly and say that within every man is the innate desire to lead. God made him to be the head. Everything in our society battles that positioning of a man, but the fact is that when Abraham was called "lord" by Sarah, that title was the greatest compliment of his life. If a wife doesn't see enough of God in her relationship with her husband to call him "lord," then that marriage has problems. Her first understanding of God in the flesh should be her husband in a relationship given by the Holy Spirit. If spiritual understanding does not start in the marriage relationship, we have a tendency either to reject spiritual authority in the Church or to cleave to it to such a degree that we justify not trusting the marriage relationship. Both are wrong.

I say by permission of the Holy Spirit that until we address relationships with maturity, the Kingdom of God cannot be finally established. The Kingdom of God is not only enhanced by relationships, it is birthed in relationships. Jesus said, "The basis of life is loving God with all your heart, and your neighbor as yourself." Paul uses the example of the husband and wife in a God-given relationship to such a degree that he implies, "Christ can come again when we become His mature, responsive Bride." This relationship between Christ and the Church is a mystery. One of the greatest mysteries of creation is the relationship between a husband and his wife in a mature, God-given relationship.

For that reason, the enemy comes in subtle ways to destroy relationships. The cry of my spirit has been for God to give my ministry some couples to whom I can send other couples who have lost their way. These couples will minister healing because they have been through the same storms. They can say, "We did not think there was a way out, but we made it." I yearn for just a few couples who have been on a rocky path and felt destruction, but by God's help and spiritual leadership, have made it. I want to have intensive counseling and therapy where I can sit people down with these trusted couples and say, "You tell them how you walked through those situations."

This letter is an indication of that beginning in counseling. If this vulnerability is honored and respected, this could be the firstfruit of a ministry that God will raise up. Most vulnerability in group counseling only engenders sexual abnormalities. Many philosophical and psychological counseling groups only engender more frustrations in marriages. But to walk through a spiritually healed, divinely anointed relationship that has experienced victory is the only way God can give us concrete examples to say, "Look! It works!"

A young person said to me the other day, "Pastor, I can number on my hand the couples whom I believe are examples to me in marriage." I grieved over that observation. Christian marriages need healing. Young people in difficulties should learn to address the real issues causing their problems. What are the real issues of their relationships? When we address these issues, we begin to live as Kingdom prototypes.

God is urging me to press His people in the area of relationships. I am not suggesting that people go back and try to resurrect old relationships that have ended, and sometimes involve other marriages. Some doors have indeed been closed. But many of God's people live in shaky areas in their existing relationships. They need to address the real issues of their lives before it is too late.

4

POSITIVE THINKING AND POSITIVE LIVING

I asked God to give me insight concerning the subject of human sexuality because I believe solutions in most areas of human life come only from God. I do not believe the mind of reason can uncover the answers to human needs in certain areas. Many of our own solutions work only temporarily. We must open ourselves to the Holy Spirit to understand God's eternal ways.

Human sexuality has to do with understanding a father's relationship with his son or daughter. It brings importance to a mother's relationship with her children. Sometimes because of the lack of proper parental relationships, emotional problems in relating to others develop in one's later years. Many influences contrib-

ute to human responsiveness in intimacy. Intimacy
between human beings develops from various needs at
various times in our lives. All people have the need for
personal intimacy. Intimacy does not always mean
sexual expression. We all need to be close enough to
other human beings to enjoy close relationships. Some
dimensions of intimacy even include people of our
same sex.

I say by permission of the Holy Spirit that sometimes
fathers who are overly affectionate with their sons,
kissing them in the mouth, for instance, can create
feelings in them which later may be expressed in
homosexual tendencies. Respect is important in a relationship between a father and his son. To stir up sexuality through excessive, even abusive, affections can
create problems in later years in a person's sexual
orientation.

I believe that a mother should be deliberate and dedicated in mothering her children. A special relationship
needs to exist between a mother and her son. Physical
expressions that begin in little boys in the early years
should primarily be directed between a mother and her
son, not the father and the son. Parental tenderness
from both parents is always proper, but physical
expressions must be channeled in the right direction
and be appropriate for the age of the child.

I believe a daughter's closeness to her father is very
important. A loving husband becomes a lifelong extension of a close relationship between a father and his
daughter. If that closeness between them is missing in
a girl's early years, something is lost in her self-
concept. Fathers must diligently seek to create close
relationships with their children. Loving relationships

in the family create the basis by which we discern the feelings of proper relationships throughout life. Securities in life are first established in our relationships in our homes.

Single parents must look to the church to make up emotional voids for themselves and their children. Mature Christians in a church must be very open in expressing love to those needing close relationships not provided by their natural families. This sensitivity insures that all members in the Body of Christ may grow properly.

How do we extend positive thinking into positive living? How do we extend positive attitudes to actual implementation in our relationships? A person's concept of God, himself and others is not necessarily what they are in reality. They seem to be whatever we believe they are. A person's opinions about God does not change Him. "God" in any person's mind is not what He actually is in reality. He is to us what we think Him to be. That is the reason Solomon said, "As he (man) thinks in his heart, so is he" (Proverbs 23:7).

God may be a God of miracles, but unless we have faith, He is not a God of miracles to us. Our opinions don't change God's miraculous power. We limit Him by our own thought processes. Apply these thoughts at a lower level in human relationships. We are who we think we are, not the person we actually are. Regardless of a person's potential, if that person has limited himself by certain negative thought processes, he will never realize his total potential. The other extreme is to think more highly of oneself, beyond any rational possibility. Presumptions invite failure and insanity in extreme cases. Insane people may believe that they are the King of England or Jesus Christ. Somewhere between those two extremes lies the potential of ourselves which God wills in our thought processes.

Let me develop "thought potential" with a story of Tom Sawyer. When Tom Sawyer got into difficulty, he would threaten his foes with a big brother who did not exist. Tom's big brother so existed in his own thought processes that he took courage in thinking, "I have a big brother to protect me." When we understand this principle, we realize that many people are not fulfilled in their lives because of the way they think about themselves. They never relate to others because they fix thought patterns around someone and that person becomes that fixed image to them.

Sometimes a husband doesn't give his wife a chance to grow because he enslaves her to thought processes that he created concerning her role. A wife may have fixed her husband in a certain thought pattern of his being "inconsiderate" or "stingy." Jesus always dealt with people's thoughts. Following His example, we must address ourselves not in terms of who we are, but by acknowledging who we think we are. We must learn how to extend positive thinking about ourselves and others to positive reality.

Across the years I have dealt with men who thought their wives were immoral when I knew that they were not. I was absolutely convinced by discernment in counseling that these women were faithful to their husbands. Because a husband had determined in his mind that his wife had been unfaithful, she was unfaithful as far as he was concerned. He gave her no opportunity to defend herself. I have seen the same situation many more times when a wife thought her husband was unfaithful. She so believed that her husband had been unfaithful to her that she fixed an image of his infidelity in her own mind. She became absolutely passive and cold toward him. In her mind, he was guilty.

God's ways usually take us to extremes in trust to maintain right relationships. It is far better to think good of someone when they are wrong than to think wrong of someone when they are good. Our thoughts about ourselves determine who we really are.

I am convinced that drug abuse can be very detrimental to self-concepts. The mental distortions of drug users convince them that they are Superman who can jump out of ten-story buildings. Drugs sometimes make a person act more passively or more aggressively than he normally would. Even taking prescription drugs should be covered by spiritual authority in the church to prevent openness in areas of wrong thought processes. I am convinced spirits are associated with medication. Any use of drugs should be presented to pastors for prayer and covering by the person taking the medication. Some people will criticize this admonition and say it is extreme, but I know this truth will stand the test of time.

Many elderly people who have been Christians all their lives are not the people we thought they were. In their later years they pursue a path of passiveness in their minds so that internally they become someone other than the strong personalities they once were. We become the person we think ourselves to be. That is the reason that we must have proper thoughts in relationships.

When we first meet people, we automatically begin to form opinions about them which may be totally untrue. Perhaps an individual favors someone else whom we do not like. Immediately, we do not like that person either. Someone looks like a person's mother, and all of a sudden that person feels warm toward that lady even though he does not know the reason. Past experiences have created an acceptable image. We must learn how to avoid making quick decisions about people. Quick judgments are characteristic of spiritually immature Christians.

Sometimes I say to couples in counseling sessions, "Suppose you were to go to a party with your slate wiped clean of all the hurts of the past. If you saw this man(woman) you now want to divorce, the chances are that you would be attracted to him(her). You are basically the same person you have always been. If you did not know all his(her) faults, failures and inadequacies, you would probably like to meet this person." Sometimes, by approaching their emotional ambivalence from that original concept, the couple open their disappointments to give and receive forgiveness. When forgiveness is genuine, a couple can reach a place where the slate can actually be so clean that they find renewed attractiveness to each other and begin the courting process all over again.

Some women work because they do not trust their husbands' abilities to supply their needs. Far too many women work for the wrong reasons. They do not know how to integrate themselves into their husbands' lives or trust their husbands' abilities to provide for the family. Divorce would be less of an alternative to the problems in a marriage if women were not so self-sufficient.

Most divorced people, including Christians, gave up on their marriages too quickly. They were not willing to give their marriages a fair chance because they formed unchangeable opinions about their mates. If they only knew that many times the people they will meet in the future will have worse traits than the partners they are leaving. People need to grow up and learn how to think properly about themselves and each other. We need to learn how to keep people out of our own mental "boxes" when they need freedom to be themselves.

We must correct our negative thought processes. How do we deal with our thoughts? The first thought process which needs correction is our personal perceptions of ourselves. "Who am I?" Every decision we make about ourselves relates directly to what and who we think we are. If we do not trust ourselves, we can never build trusting relationships.

We must learn Christian discipline before we can ever trust others. If we cannot pursue discipline in our own appetites, we won't ever completely trust other people to keep their promises to us. We will always have a problem with trust in relationships. We may never know the real reasons, but we will always think that somebody is throwing us a curve. We have to begin with the ability to know who we are and to handle our own lives. Only then can we ever enjoy mature relationships.

Perception of others is an extension of self-perception. Many people never reach the maturity to understand that principle. They spend their lives accusing others of being "stubborn" or "immoral." They always try to blame others when their problems actually begin with their own self-perceptions.

What would be our attitude toward a situation that involves sex outside of a covenant relationship? Why do we accept Christian morality? Do we accept morality because it is convenient, a covering, or because we really believe that it is right? All of the answers to these questions relate to who we actually are inside.

A good counselor knows that when one starts accusing a partner, he(she) immediately gives clues as to what he(she) thinks of himself. Jesus pointed out that people who judge others always have similar offenses in their own lives (Matthew 6:1-5). Those who always accuse others of some offense usually are having problems in that same area. Those who continuously preach about immorality usually have morality problems in their own thoughts. We expose ourselves by what we think about others.

Secondly, Christians must have proper thought processes about the subject of marriage or covenant relationships. We must always recognize that without God's approval and blessings, marriages are doomed to failure. The first chapter of Genesis says God created man, male and female. In that relationship, He made them halves of one another which together make a whole unit. Then God blessed them. He did not bless them separately. He blessed them in oneness. We cannot receive the full blessings of God until we are in proper relationships with others. Jesus said, ". . . for he who does not love his brother whom he has seen, how can he love God whom he has not seen?" (I John 4:20). This understanding demands spiritual maturity.

Without proper relationships, we receive only partial blessings from God. When we are in right relationships, God can pour out His blessings and we have spiritual confidence. We know who we are and the purposes, motives and goals of our lives.

An example of the consequences of a broken spiritual relationship is seen in the life of Judas. When Judas lost his relationship with Jesus and the disciples, he ended his life in suicide. Why do people contemplate suicide? Suicide is an extreme result of wrong motivations in relationships. The blessings of God cannot flow. People who contemplate suicide feel isolated and cut off from others. Loneliness is a result of cutting off relationships which God wills for us to develop.

Closing off all relationships except for that with a husband or a wife gives insufficient fulfillment. If a marriage is whole and healthy, it not only handles other close relationships, those relationships prosper and feed that marriage. I am not condoning extramarital sexual intimacy, I am referring to other God-given relationships in addition to the covenant commitment in marriage. As long as a woman thinks she is being raped every time a man puts his hand on her shoulder, she is in trouble. If she thinks a man wants to go to bed with her every time he looks straight into her eyes, she has problems. And yet that thinking exists in every Christian church.

Some people will try to take advantage of Christian relationships. Any pastor knows those situations are common because he deals regularly with them in counseling. But because we have a few exceptions in every church which create problems, we cannot reject the opportunity from God to build close relationships. We must learn how to both accept and give affection.

If we love our children and think they can do no

wrong, but we think that all other children are aggravating, mean and ugly, we have problems being objective in our thoughts. For example, here is a test. If our own child goes into the living room, eats popcorn and scatters it all over the carpet, we may clean it up and possibly never even correct him. Yet when a neighbor's child does the same thing, we wait until his mother is not around to jerk him by the arm and say, "Don't drop popcorn on my floor!" That behavior reveals a thought process problem.

Everything I am addressing has to do with sexuality. Sexuality is confirmation and expression of inward thought processes. Intimacy is an expression of ongoing relationships which can grow to give total and complete satisfaction.

The third area in which we must correct our thought processes is in knowing the purpose of sex. How many times have we heard that food is the way to a man's heart? We have all heard the old saying, "The way to a man's heart is through his stomach." Ridiculous! A man can get food in a cafeteria! We play games with our minds. The way to a man's heart is when he becomes so integrated with his wife that they totally know one another.

Sex can be improperly used for wrong motives and harmful purposes. Sex can be used to gain some ultimate end, but the victory will be short-lived and unfulfilling. When sex is fulfilling, it is God-given to develop and maintain closeness in the relationship. A good sexual relationship is probably one of the most sustaining, refreshing experiences known to mankind. Many times we are unaware of what provisions God has made to refresh us.

When we don't understand God's purposes, we simply become more and more lonely and frustrated. We take out our frustrations by raiding the refrigerator, doing abnormal exercises to develop muscles, running further or more often than we should, or by over-shopping. All of these activities are expressions of frustrations, even of frustrated sexuality. None of these activities are necessary for us to be the complete, total people whom God intends for us to be.

The fourth area in which our thinking must be corrected is captured in one little word: "belong." If we have to remind a man(woman) that he(she) belongs to us, that relationship is very unstable. To think that we own a husband or a wife because we have a legal contract is probably the greatest misunderstanding of the purpose of marital relationships. A person cannot be forced to belong to someone because at some point in their lives they signed a contract. A person can be forced only to live out the letter of the law. We belong to those people who bring us completion and fulfillment. To attempt to force a relationship to uphold a contractual agreement is a tragic mistake. The Word of God says, "He who swears to his own hurt, and does not change" (Psalms 15:4). Too many marriages are living under a contractual agreement. The couple have sworn to their own hurts, "for better or for worse."

A person can learn how to cope with circumstances which demand mature acceptance. But when the couple begin at an altar by saying, "Well, this marriage may be good or bad. Maybe this relationship will work out for better or for worse," that couple already have a wrong mental attitude about marriage. We need to correct any mental concept that people "belong" to other people.

Not even our children "belong" to us. Parents may force their children to come straight home from school, to wear certain kinds of shoes or to go to Sunday school, but children do not belong to their parents at all. They belong to the person who fulfills them, who answers their questions about life and gives them secure relationships which allow them to grow.

Another area in which we need to have proper thought patterns is in making the distinction between love and trust. Love is a characteristic that is God-like within us. We can love the unlovable. I am convinced that many people divorce companions out of love for them. They see their companions terribly unhappy and unfulfilled. Those companions are never able to be content in their relationships. Down deep inside, a husband or wife will say, "I love you so much that I want to release you." Right or wrong, this motive is often in our thought processes. A relationship does not last in love alone. Relationships last in trust. Trust is not something we can just give to someone. Trust must always be earned.

I have learned that we can promise to give someone trust, but trust must be earned by consistency. Trust— not love—is the basis of proper sexuality. A person can give himself in some cheap sexual experience with someone he doesn't love, trust or know. But we cannot maintain a growing, intimate relationship with someone without trust. It cannot be done. We can have a relationship that gives sexual pleasure as long as we build it up in fantasy or bring other thought processes to bed, but I promise that relationship will run out of steam. Proper responses in intimacy are born out of trust. No woman can give herself emotionally to a man whom she does not trust. No man can give himself consistently to a woman whom he does not trust. It is that simple.

I want to share another letter which expresses the necessity of trust in developing a growing, satisfying intimacy:

"My lover, my honey and my friend. I have decided to be vulnerable. You asked me from the very beginning of our relationship to trust you. As we were youngsters getting married, we had a very shallow view of relationships based on trust. What is trust anyway? Because you are the man and supposedly my head, you are 'the king.' But are you worthy of my trust because you are male? What of me? Am I really so dumb and irrational, illogically created and therefore not to be trusted?

"I hear so much preaching and teaching about this matter of trust: 'Trust is earned. Trust is the only way to submission. Until you trust someone, you will never trust God.' You have broken my trust. It will take time to allow it to grow again. You will have to earn it back.

"Money, money, money and trust. I know that money is the main issue of our problems, my darling. I want to trust you so completely. Something deep inside of me tells me to let go and allow you to rule me. I could trust you again, but I am afraid I will lose my personhood and my right to think and have opinions. If I completely let you run our lives, how will I have my own voice or opinions? How can I trust you to give me all of my needs and desires?

"Sometimes, in the quietness of the night, I long to tell you of my deepest fears and how inadequate I feel. I long to tell you how much I need you, but I do not believe you would listen to me with

87

your heart. I am afraid you will patronize me and tell me, 'That is nice. Yes, honey,' and act as if you understand when you really don't.

"When I was a little girl, I can remember telling my parents how other children were able to buy ice cream at school. I wanted to buy ice cream, too, but my parents would not give me the money for ice cream. I can remember feeling so misunderstood. I became convinced they did not trust me or they would believe how badly I wanted ice cream.

"I began to steal the money. After I stole money the first time, I found it was easy, so I did it again and again. Then I began to lie. That was easy, too. I no longer had to trust my parents for my needs. I could now get things I wanted my own way.

"Then I got a job because of my own self-reliance. Honey, how am I supposed to trust you when I do not even trust myself? How can I be submissive to you and make you my spiritual head? To trust you with money is very difficult for me. I am humiliated to come to ask for money from you. I am afraid you won't believe my need for the money is valid. These feelings churn inside me sometimes. Then when it is time for sex with you, I find myself fearful of your controlling me.

"Then I don't believe that you understand my feelings or my emotions, and you are only interested in getting sexual pleasure and personal gratification.

"I do not trust your motives. When I ask you to share them with me—your emotions, your feelings—you back away. Why is it so hard for you to share your feelings and thoughts with me?

"I want to share everything with you. Sometimes I feel like you are really interested in all my thoughts and fears, and other times you are not. What difference does it make? I get confused with the standards you set for our children when I see you breaking those standards yourself.

"Sweetheart, I long for you to take me in your arms and pray with me. Why is it so hard for us to be vulnerable to each other before God? Are we afraid of His light on our relationship? Sometimes I believe it is all due to exhaustion and laziness. Who is in charge of our prayer life? I am trying to trust you. I am not sure if I even know what I can do to earn your trust at its deepest level.

"Sweetheart, I believe trust is when we feel that we can share any feelings, thoughts, doubts, fears, joys or sadness and have a total sense of knowing that we will not be rejected. I believe an added dimension is knowing each other so well and so completely that when situations arise, I will know exactly how you will respond. I believe in the honesty that such a relationship could achieve. I want that for us. Sweetheart, I want to submit to you and trust you so that you will meet my desires according to God's will. I want to see you as my 'lord' and be able to transfer that reverence to the heavenly Father.

"I want that trust for our children. I know that they will only trust us and God at the level that we lead them. My dad broke my trust. I know he made mistakes which have left me wounded and confused. Your parents did the same to you.

"Please don't stop 'courting' me. Somehow when we dated, I trusted you more. I believed you could do no wrong and I believed you felt the same about me. I know life is not always fun, but I sure do miss that part of our relationship. I long to be courted first, and then go to the next step to sexual intercourse, and then to prayer. First comes the relationship, then comes the intimacy, and finally comes the ability to enjoy total oneness before God.

"You don't call me or ask me out for dates anymore. I feel as if you want sex without romance. What good is sex without romance? I felt totally different the times we laughed and shared together and then had sex, compared to the times when we tried

89

to foreplay.

"I love you, I am glad we are growing and that I can share this letter with you. I believe in us and I trust God in both of us to give answers to our hearts' deepest questions."

As men become the spiritual authority in their homes they may seem to lead their wives around by the nose for awhile. If those men are not leading their wives in the right spiritual paths, they will eventually wonder what happened to their intimacy. Though she may not have told him, intimacy fails when a wife doesn't trust her husband's decisions. Trust is built in the ability to say, "My husband will hear from God or he won't act. If he doesn't hear from God on his own, he will go to a spiritual authority and together they will hear from God."

Relationships rest in our confidence in one another. The world spends millions and millions of dollars keeping surface sexuality alive. The Hollywood mentality insists that if someone doesn't have a dozen affairs, he is a total failure at romance. Sex is meaningless. Kingdom people will become prototypes in relationships to the world when we learn to live out Kingdom principles in relationships.

The first requirement for an intimate relationship in marriage is knowing one another. The Bible in both the Old and New Testaments uses the term, "knew." "Abraham 'knew' his wife and she bore a child." The greatest compliment that I can have from my Presbytery is for one of them to say, "This is what Bishop Paulk would do." I want to live with them so closely that any one of them would act in any situation just as I would. You say, "That thinking is conceited." Paul said to those who followed him in the ministry, "Watch me and do whatever I do."

Blessings do not come directly from God to us. They come through us at whatever level of intimacy we enjoy in a relationship with God. Jesus said, "Pray, 'Our Father.' " He could have called God, "You in the sky," but He didn't. He knew that a good fatherly relationship opens the door to understanding the character of the eternal Father and His desire to love us. Think of the boys and girls who cannot comfortably pray, "Our Father," because of poor relationships with their own fathers.

Mechanical sexual foreplay is immature. Lovemaking is never an academic exercise. In mature relationships which are already intact, sexual intimacy becomes a matter of simply physically expressing love. Someone says, "I have been reading this book on how to find the love zones of a woman. I have finally learned the secret. You touch her here, and that does it." That information is totally ridiculous. The secret to intimacy is understanding feelings inside of a woman and a man. What brings her security? What brings him fulfillment?

Indeed, trust is the key to intimacy. Trust is earned through consistency—doing the same things ourselves that we demand of others. Trust is born in spirituality. We cannot ever separate good daily relationships from proper sexual responses.

The letter from this woman deals basically with trust. That is the reason I chose to share it in this study. What is trust? Does being a man make someone worthy of trust? Does manhood make him worthy of headship?

"Submit to me because I'm your husband"? No, a woman submits because her husband is trustworthy. Until we trust someone in a God-given relationship, we will never trust God.

The writer of this letter said, "I want to trust you so completely. Something within me says to 'let go' and let you rule me." Until we reach that place, we will never enjoy a total and complete sexual relationship. Paul said, "Your own body does not belong to you." That principle not only corrects our minds but also releases us to the fullest degree to involve ourselves totally and completely in a covenant relationship. Until that happens, sex is only an experience for the moment. Sex is then similar to masturbation. Even rape exists within marriage. Because two people have a license on the wall, it does not solve their problems with freedom in intimacy.

Sexual perversion is rampant in our society. Why is there such perversion and exploitation today concerning adults having sex with children? One of the biggest pornographic markets today involves a demand for pictures of little children having sex with adults. Why? The reason is that those exploitive adults are afraid to have mature relationships with other adults. Most of those perverted relationships come about through fear of failure at having sex with an adult partner. This abberation creates a false sense of secure pleasure which brings gratification for a moment. This lust is very dangerous. Our children must be warned about the possibility of physical expolitation in a society which demands that they exercise caution against physical abusers.

The Bible said of Joseph that he refused pleasure for a season. Seasonal pleasures are born out of sins that excite the flesh but never touch the Spirit. These sins are the root motivation for people who have sex with animals which is a very common thing. Even the Bible speaks about this sin (Leviticus 18:23). People indulge sexually for a moment to gain physical gratification which does not demand that they give themselves in relationships. A lot of psychologically sick men and women indulge in this practice, yet most of them never address their real problems.

The reason that pornographic materials are so popular is that many people need some outside mental stimulation to produce a physical response. A stimulus from an outside source cannot be realized in actual relationships. Giving of oneself to someone else is inadequate satisfaction. Instead, pornography produces a cheap turn-on. Physical gratification from pornography never lasts. It only leads to mental problems, broken relationships and often suicidal tendencies.

A tremendous misunderstanding exists in society concerning the root causes of homosexuality. The gay community is increasing today and has become acceptable because it is large enough to demand some social and political acceptance. But for the most part, people who are pulled into the homosexual subculture are not gay because they choose to be. I am not implying—as some people contend—that homosexuality is inborn. We all are born with the potential of cultivating masculine or feminine traits. A person's sexual orientation begins with socially gratifying influences in the early years. Many homosexuals are very sensitive, creative people whose basic problem is less sexual than social.

93

Homosexual orientation begins with a person's inability to compete in the sexual identity of his(her) own gender. Homosexuality begins with a little boy's feelings that a man's world is too competitive, or not typically in his areas of interests. Sometimes an inept mother may not understand how to create the right kinds of interests for her son. She makes his world more feminine than masculine. He finds that he can compete with feminine values while the masculine world is too difficult for him to achieve success. He thinks, "Why not try something that is feminine?"

I am going to say something for which I run the risk of being misunderstood. Every male hairdresser is definitely not a homosexual, but that sort of occupation requires skills that both men and women can do well. Interior decorating or fashion designing are areas a man can enter and compete professionally without being sexually identified. He doesn't face masculine competition as he would if he were a carpenter, a bricklayer or a pipefitter.

Women today are more readily entering professions traditionally identified as "masculine." I realize that many women argue that they choose these professions for the high salaries, but sexual identification is still a central issue in that choice. Women working in construction or as firefighters, for instance, have chosen a "man's world" to perform physically beyond social demands. Again, not all women in traditionally "masculine" professions are lesbians by any means, but they should carefully examine the reasons and the gratifying motives for their choices. Perhaps they were more comfortable in their father's "world" than their mother's. Perhaps they were rewarded more for chopping wood" with dad than "going shopping" with mother.

For Christians to point an accusing finger at a homosexual is cruel. Most people who find themselves caught between these two worlds are very sensitive and often very creative. They don't know what to do with their feelings. Many times they only know that they prefer sewing to pouring concrete. They would far rather be styling hair than driving a tractor. Until we understand these differences in their preferences, a Christian community can never help those in bondage to homosexuality. When the gay community finds out how well Christians can handle dealing with their problems, ministries to those wishing to come out of the homosexual community, such as "Such Were Some of You" ministries, will not even be able to accommodate the overwhelming response. Homosexuals do not feel comfortable competing with those of their own sex. They cope with life by living in a sexual orientation that can never really bring them satisfaction.

Someone says, "My husband bakes cakes, and he has no homosexual tendencies." That may be true. Baking may be an expression of a world in which he had approval as a little boy. Perhaps the first time he received approval for an achievement was when he helped his mother in the kitchen. Now as an adult, his approval and satisfaction still come from that world. Perhaps his dad neglected to take him out to cut grass or to give him approval for doing a good job fixing the car. We must grow mature enough to say, "Well, so what! Why not allow men to compete in a feminine world but not express it sexually?" When sexual gratification is attached to feeling proud of our achieve ments, that satisfaction creates a lifestyle.

Until we understand this correlation, we will never know how to nurture our children properly. Many ministries are trying to cast out spirits when they should be praying over parents to properly channel their children's values. Someone says, "Well, a domineering mother creates a homosexual son." That is not necessarily true. Perhaps that mother approved her son in the wrong areas. A man may also reject his son in the wrong areas. Because a little boy is not an expert in a man's world, he feels inadequate and rejected by his father. He backs away saying, "Mom, can I sweep the kitchen for you?"

Until we learn how to handle our thought processes, we will never address our problems properly. As long as we look at certain people as being evil and attribute a "Sodom and Gomorrah" mentality to them, we will never be able to help them.

Homosexuality can be caused by the fear of failure in competition with the same sex or even the fear of sex itself. Many women adopt lesbian tendencies because they did not have good, sexual relationships with their husbands early in their marriages. Maybe a husband did not know how to bring out his wife's sexuality. As a result, she began to channel strong feelings toward another woman. Where is the failure in this? Who is to blame? Homosexuality continues in a person's life because sexual pleasure comes from the wrong sources. Maybe the first sexual expressions began with little boys or little girls playing together. Some children are never quite able to trust their desires for the opposite sex.

Of course, sexual intimacy is never blessed by God

outside of a covenant relationship. But sometimes, even within marriage, the motivation for sexual expression is sinful and abusive. Selfish intentions never bring sexual satisfaction. Certain motivations are always wrong in sexual intimacy.

Sex is sinful when it demeans or physically abuses another person. Sex is wrong if it makes another person feel less than a valuable creation of God.

Sex is sinful or evil when it is used selfishly, only for physical gratification and personal convenience.

Sex is wrong when it does not contribute to the proper self-image of someone else. A partner is left feeling ugly, dirty and used instead of feeling special to someone.

Sex is also sinful when spirits control the act of sexuality. This driving force is the sin of Sodom and Gommorah. Lust is a spirit. When lust controls a relationship, the relationship is driven. Sex becomes a demanding, forceful compulsion in the relationship because spirits drive people to action. If a person has to move sexually every few hours, that person is driven by spirits. It can be absolutely normal to have sex every day, but it can also be very normal not to do so. Sexual activity cannot be set by a gauge, clock or a calendar. Sexual frequency varies according to the relationship.

When spirits control a sexual act, sex is sinful to its fullest degree. Spirits will cause someone to rape or kill. Sometimes spirits control at another dimension when someone forces the other person in some way. Spirits control when there is a tendency or desire to hurt someone. When someone gets turned on by making a partner scream or bruises on a partner's body, sex is sinful. A great misunderstanding of sexuality is the desire to leave a "passion mark" on someone's neck. The end of that road is rape because spirits have become involved. When a person cannot look into a lover's eyes to love them and receive satisfaction through tenderness, he(she) has spiritual problems. If a person cannot say, "I am loving you," when he(she) is making love, they are not "making love." Sex becomes an act of self-gratification.

Many women have said to me in counseling, "He tries to make love to me, yet he never says a word. I just want him to whisper to me, 'Honey, I love you.' " Don't allow spirits to drive a relationship because they will never be satisfied. They must always experiment to find a new thrill. If someone must stand on his(her) head to make love, that person is driven. Having sex in more than one position is not sinful, but if someone requires extreme, excessive variety to find sexual satisfaction, that demand indicates the activity of driving spirits rather than the spirit of a covenant relationship based on love.

I conclude by proposing that the key to fulfilled Christian sexuality is extending positive thinking into positive living. I give three suggestions on how to do this. Until thought patterns are proper, we cannot change our living patterns. Positive living starts in our thought processes. The attitudes in our thoughts control us. That is the reason Mammon rules in the thought processes and always motivates ungodly reasoning processes, security, obsessions and choices of lifestyles.

The first step we must take to go from positive thinking to positive living is to know God's sovereign will for our lives. Unless our expressions of sexuality relate to a God-given call or position in life, positive living will always be hindered.

The second suggestion is to learn the power of prayer. Most people pray without knowing the power of prayer. In the Garden of Gethsemane when Jesus prayed, "Thy will be done," He reached a climactic relationship with His Father. When we reach a place where we can say, "I want your will, not mine," we can have total and complete satisfaction in our love for someone else.

A husband can say, "This is for you, honey. I am so sensitive to your needs that every move I make is to satisfy you." Impossible? Oh, no! But true oneness happens only in the lives of couples who respect and know God, and live in spiritual submission to Him and to each other. A Christian wife cannot submit to a husband, even sexually, until she understands the principle of spiritual submission. Oneness is the total and complete climactic expression of submission in the flesh. The cheap counterfeit of oneness is that sexuality which drives an individual in a way that he(she) will never be completely satisfied.

Finally, moving from positive thinking to positive living requires diligence. Don't give up. If a relationship is not growing, the reason is probably a lack of trust. The most beautiful way that a relationship reaches total fulfillment is to begin at whatever point couples are, and move toward total fullfillment as couples grow together. If couples are not better lovers after ten or fifteen years of marriage than they were in the beginning, they still don't understand intimacy. The more two people become integrated and know one another, the more they are able to express and receive total fulfillment as God intended.

5

HOME SWEET HOME

God is exhorting Christian families today, "Get your house in order!" Clearly, the spiritual responsibility for covering and leadership of a family flows first to a godly husband and father. But spiritual headship for a family extends to both a husband and a wife who are in a right relationship under God. A husband in a covenant relationship will know how to submit to his wife under many appropriate conditions. The creation that God blessed in the first chapter of Genesis was a man, both male and female. While individuality may be expressed in two separate personalities, a husband and wife together in covenant with God comprise total headship.

Explaining the Godhead is impossible because the Trinity is a mystery. We know that God is One, but we see Him expressed in three distinct personalities. We see God expressed in His Fatherhood, in the work of the Holy Spirit, and in the incarnation of the Son. If we already possessed the immortal body that Jesus had as part of the Trinity, Jesus' incarnation into flesh would have been unnecessary.

As the Godhead is One, yet expressed in three distinct personalities, a man and woman in headship are also one. A man has certain responsibilities to God, just as a woman has certain God-given responsibilities. Together they become the image of God and demonstrate true headship and true authority. Headship is destroyed when one partner assumes the role of the other or takes away from the other partner's role.

Stereotyped roles in dividing household chores have no place in marriages when the man and woman are both working. If both partners work outside the home, I believe that a man should be just as responsible for cooking and washing dishes as his wife. Cutting grass is just as appropriate for the wife as for the husband. The only reason that some tasks are more appropriate for one partner or the other is that she may be a better cook and he may enjoy yard work more. However, a couple should be in agreement as to which chores each one prefers and can do best.

A man who has great physical dexterity might be better at cutting grass than his wife. My wife, Norma, takes out the garbage perhaps only twice a year. Do you know who takes out the garbage at our house? I do! Someone may say, "I didn't know senior pastors did that." Oh, yes! Do you know who uses the vacuum cleaner at our house? I do! I know that some people have accused me of being a "male chauvinist" who does not understand liberated women, but I do understand. I understand headship from a personal perspective. I also know how and when to submit to a spiritual woman, and I have no problem with that at all.

Unfortunately, many women's rights groups do not want to acknowledge God's divine order. They totally demolish the male role from God's intentions concerning headship. They do not want male distinctions in authority to be necessary or recognized. That attitude bothers me for many reasons.

In right relationships, God always blesses headship in the family. However, specific areas of headship are never the same in two different households. When my wife and I have steaks at our house, I cook them. I am so glad to get them, I willingly cook them! When we cook chicken on the grill, I do the cooking. I am not good at baking bread, however. The last time I tried to bake bread was when I was seventeen years old. That bread turned out to be much too hard because I used baking soda instead of something else I was supposed to use. My family never gave me another chance to bake again.

Learn individual strengths within a family unit and do not say, "Well, I don't approve of the way that family lives over there. She does this and he does that." Leave other couples to their own living arrangements! As long as they have a good working relationship in covenant with God, they will demonstrate headship.

Many women are better bookkeepers than their husbands. Some men think that they should carry the checkbook around simply because they are the "head" of the household. With that reasoning, some couples will end up in bankruptcy. If a wife knows better how to handle the finances, let her be responsible for them and serve that vital role in headship. But if a husband knows better how to handle money, he should be in charge. We are eventually going to realize that God has common sense. He is not ignorant when He puts two people together in marriage.

Families who are out of God's divine order open themselves to encounter many problems, and their relationships cannot possibly honor or please God. Problems in relationships are often the first indication that family headship is out of order. For the sake of family relationships, parents should be in firm agreement concerning their children's discipline. That principle is important to implement in every family. Children will never understand submission to any authority or direction from spiritual authority unless they see unity in parental discipline. If Daddy says, "No, you cannot go to the movies tonight," and the child runs to ask his mother's permission, knowing she will say, "Yes, sure you can go," that child will have many problems with authority throughout his life. For that reason, I suggest parents agree on a final checkpoint in the family.

If a husband agrees that he wants his wife to give final permission to their children's activities, and he will support her judgments, then I will not argue with their decision. However, I do not think that plan works best for most families. God created differences in the basic strengths of a man and a woman. The ability to make quick decisions without emotional reactions is not typical of a woman's character.

Usually a man has more of a "computer" mind, and a woman is more of a "feeler." She has the ability to comfort and counsel. She has certain innate abilities which make her a good discerner of truth. A woman's "intuition" lifted to its highest level is spiritual discernment. We must learn each other's strengths and trust each other's God-given abilities.

If a wife is a better "decision-maker" than her husband, and he is willing to submit to her decisions, their roles are pleasing to God. But a woman is out of order to try to assume that "final decision" role presumptuously. I believe that wives should encourage their husbands to make the final decisions in their families.

I must emphasize again the absolute importance of parental agreement in matters concerning their children. The worst mistake parents can make is to argue over the family's decisions in front of their children. At certain ages, parental disagreement causes a child's world to crumble. Divorce is very cruel for children. Many people from divorced families are emotionally scarred for years without understanding the root causes. They do not realize that their constant emotional pain is caused from the trauma of their parents' divorce years ago. During that period of their lives, their worlds fell apart. The people they had trusted most no longer loved one another and could no longer live together.

When I was a little boy, I remember times when I felt tension between my mother and dad. Those times caused me great anxiety. In the Word of the Lord, we find examples of devastation to families when parents are in disagreement. For instance, Isaac and his wife, Rebekah, got into disagreements over whether Jacob or Esau would receive the blessing. Esau was older and by legal right should have received it, but he sold his right of the blessing to Jacob.

Without going into the details of the story, I simply want to emphasize that the parents, Isaac and Rebekah, were in disagreement. Mother plotted with Jacob, "Take some kind of fur skin and put on your arms. Tell your dad, who has failing eyesight, that you are Esau." Rebekah's advice was deception to that family, and that is the reason Jacob is called "the deceiver." Yet in the plan of God, Jacob was the one whom God chose to receive His blessings.

Children learn deception when their parents are in disagreement. Years later, Jacob and Esau met in a field where Jacob expected Esau would try to kill him. Cain slew Abel after Eve had deceptively usurped Adam's authority. Because headship was out of order, mankind lost fellowship with God. A "house out of order" always brings about rebellion, resentment and hostility. The children of such a household will always express those attitudes.

I recently talked with one of the most rebellious young men I have ever met. I loved him desperately. I tried to jog him, even frighten him out of his rebellion. I tried to love him to his senses. I tried everything that I knew to reach him in the brief conversation that we had together, but I got no response from him at all. Shortly after that encounter, he lay in the hospital near death. He was doing what they described on the news as "playing chicken" and was hit by a car. That boy was so confused, he would do almost anything to get

106

attention. He particularly needed the consistent attention of a man.

Young people need to recognize the patterns of authority in the families of ones with whom they are considering marriage. Many people cannot understand the desperate needs in another person. They say, "I cannot help it. I married a cruel man." I would like to drop a little morsel of insight if I may: Do not get married quickly. Learn that person's personality and family patterns before marriage. Pastoral counseling can prevent lifelong pain and heartache, but unfortunately, some people are afraid to submit their relationships to spiritual counseling. Those people weaken their chances for successful marriages. Many people marry to get away from home or to escape personal problems. They only initiate greater conflicts. Marriage ordained by God will be beautiful, but an untimely marriage, out of God's will, can literally be hell on earth.

Like most pastors with compassionate congregations, I have a host of divorced people in my church. I address their problems out of great love for them. We never withhold truth or restoration from people who have made regrettable mistakes in marriages. They have not committed unpardonable sins. As a matter of fact, we have two divorced pastors on our Presbytery. I address divorce problems as I do problems within the homosexual community. I say tough things to them because I speak boldly in their behalf. I can make certain difficult recommendations to divorced people because they understand how much I love them.

After a divorce, parents should try to maintain a cordial relationship for the sake of their children. The couple need to pursue as much unity as possible in decisions regarding their children's lives, even if they cannot agree on any other subject. Children should never feel as if they are a battleground between their parents. They didn't ask to be born. Many were born out of lustful desires or were conceived through accidents in birth control. They do not deserve to be treated as pawns in a cruel game, growing up in frustration and confusion all their lives. Parents chose to marry, and they produced children for whom they share a joint responsibility even after a divorce.

Why is Satan's attack on families so powerfully direct today? The family unit is the first line of defense against Satan's destruction of people's lives. Proper order in a Spirit-led family presents a strong defense against Satan. Does a family need to be submitted to the church to be in proper order? God is always first. His authority in the earth, the Body of Christ, is an authority above an individual family's authority. But the family is still the first line of defense against Satan. The family has the first opportunity to train a child properly. The first thought processes, the first feelings calling for a response from a person come from his parents. A baby's first impressions of life come while he is still in his mother's womb.

However, I must add that the first opportunity Satan has to destroy an individual also rests in the family. The first destructive thought patterns begin in the family because the child has a tendency to think just as his parents think. God was not pronouncing judgment when He said He would visit the sins of the parents to the third and forth generation (Exodus 20:5); He was simply making an observation. God does not curse anyone. When someone lives a self-centered life, that person will likely teach his children to do the same.

Abused children become abusive parents. We would assume that the last person in the world to abuse a child would be someone who had been abused himself. Statistics prove otherwise. Studies show that almost all abusive parents were abused as children. Why? That pattern was established early in their lives.

Only by the power of spiritual discernment and deliverance can certain destructive thought patterns be broken. Alcoholism, the use of tobacco, and other types of bondages become so ingrained within us that they can be broken only by the power of God. Many times sustained freedom from bondages requires extensive spiritual counseling. Although counseling is never a substitute for deliverance from a demonic spirit, spiritual counseling helps to maintain one's deliverance.

The academically trained counselors in my church provide a tremendous service. No contradictions exist between a deliverance ministry and Christian academic counseling. Even physical healing through prayer does not contradict medical healing when medicine is directed by God and is not administered through humanistic or atheistic motives. Medical procedures often become tools in the hand of God. Anything that fights sin, sickness and death is God-given. God uses both spiritual gifts and medical technology to give support to life.

The family is where God gives His first call to responsibility for others. Headship is responsible for that family's welfare. I believe that all parents will stand before God and give an account for the life of every child they have not raised in accordance with the Bible's standards. Children's lives are a testimony for or against their parents' obedience to God.

A child's first experience of genuine love should be in his home. His second experience with loving people should be through the church. Love relationships in one environment should support the love experienced in another environment. Christians should extend their love for their natural families into the church. If a home breaks down in sustaining loving relationships, that family can still have the church to support them. The most immature attitude a divorced man can have is hating the church that loves his family. The worst offense a woman can commit is hating a church that loves her children and husband after she leaves them. What hope does that family have without the church? The church is a life-giving place of secure love. The church often gives the loving support that the home has never given.

If a man is going to be a teacher, deacon or elder, his home must be in submission to spiritual authority. How can a man rule in God's house if he cannot rule his own household? When a leader is actually living out the principles he teaches, we can say, "I trust that person's teaching."

I have three daughters who are now active participants in the ministry of my church and are also dedicated to the Kingdom of God. I would confidently compare their lives and ministries to those of anyone's daughters. Many people who give advice on family relationships have children who aren't even faithful to the house of God.

The family should be a prototype of the Kingdom of God. Good examples for children should be set not only in the church but in their homes as well. The church should teach the family how to be Kingdom-oriented. A father should learn proper headship and define his responsibilities of providing for his household. The mother should learn that God has given her an innate ability to comfort and to discern.

The Bible instructs husbands to be comforted at the breasts of their wives (Proverbs 5:19). A woman is made to be a solution to a man's needs. When a woman and a man are in a right relationship, their greatest comfort will be companionship found in their God-given covenant. Everything else in their circumstances may seem hopeless, but if that covenant relationship holds firm, the end result will honor that spiritual covenant with God's blessings.

A couple need to know each other so well that they can freely discuss whether it is time to make love or time to go to sleep. That decision usually should not belong to the wife. A husband will know the appropriate times to say, "You do not need to serve me. You need to go to sleep." She will trust him without feeling that she has been rejected or denied. I am talking about mature relationships. Unfortunately, those relationships are few.

Children are the seed and fruit of the love in a family. The church and the family should totally complement each other. They should never be competitive. To have the church and its headship in competition with the headship of a family causes destruction of that family. I promise that the Church is going to survive. Jesus said that the gates of hell would not stand against the

111

Church, but He did not say that about the family.

Families need to so fix their trust in a Bible-centered church that if everything else falls apart — even if the parents were killed in an accident — the children could walk into the arms of a pastor and know safety. Parents need to tell their children, "The pastors would know what to do with you, honey. You could trust them." Some parents' negative comments about the church and its pastors are absolutely destroying the possibility of life-and-death ministry if the need should arise. Those parents often don't realize the potential dangers they are planting in their children's minds.

The church and the family together find the direction of God. Together they hear the voice of God and learn how to be obedient to what God is saying. Together they know when God is speaking in circumstances. The church should be the family's hospital for spiritual needs, while the family should be the church's hospital for physical needs. I want to re-emphasize that the church and the family should totally complement one another. Security is destroyed through competitiveness.

I believe that the generation which is now in authority must pass away. I also believe that the generation who will enter into the Kingdom promise of God has now been birthed. In my spirit, I believe that potentially any generation could have been that victorious, final generation before the coming of the Lord. That generation which God has prepared is now growing and we must mature the seed properly. I see some real possibilities of that happening.

Our kindergarten class at Chapel Hill Harvester

Schools was recently visited by a medical team who came to teach the children what to do in certain kinds of emergencies. One situation had to do with someone who had been injured and required crutches. None of the children wanted to pray for that situation because if they prayed, they knew the injured person would be healed, and they wouldn't get to play with the crutches!

Another situation dealt with what they would do in case somebody died. Who would they call? What would they do if they encountered an accident where they found someone dead? The children gathered around the child who was playing dead and decided that they would raise him from the dead! Those kids are listening to what is being taught at home and in the church! For fathers and mothers not to cooperate with the church by giving support to its teaching would be a great tragedy.

I believe that the seed has already been born who can in fact live out the will of God to the extent that God can say to principalities and powers, "My Son can come again." What kept Israel from God's promises? If Israel is our example, we need to understand what kept them in the wilderness for so long. What keeps Christians from enjoying fulfilling Kingdom relationships?

The church and the family together bring God's will to pass on earth as it is in heaven. But until they work together, God's will cannot be accomplished. Sometimes I can identify with Paul when he laments, "I just want to take you in my arms and love you. I am distraught when I see you miss the mark." Some Christian people get so far off course that they lose out on God's intentions for them. God intended great things for them, but they get caught up in their own kingdoms.

We need to ask God, "What are Your intentions for my family? What are Your intentions for me in the church? What are Your intentions for me in my community?"

The home should be the first place children see good examples as role models for their lives. If they don't see examples of good character at home, how are they ever going to learn to live responsibly? How will a boy know the proper way to care for a girl if his father doesn't treat his mother respectfully? I know a boy's home environment after watching his behavior around a girl for ten minutes. I can tell what kind of home a girl comes from when I watch her behavior around a boy. Young people are an expression of their parents' behavior and attitudes.

If a parent complains that he has a rebellious son, he should ask himself where the boy learned rebellion. "My kid hates authority." Where did he learn to hate it? Perhaps that child once saw his father drive eighty miles an hour and then laugh at a policeman who couldn't catch him. Authority is authority.

Children learn by their parents' examples to respect others. That attitude is basic in a home environment. God's Word says, "You should give a tithe." If children see their parents in consistent disobedience to God, those parents will live to see disobedience emerge in their children's choices. Those parents will say, "Where did they learn that controlling attitude? Where did they learn to rebel against authority?" They learned it from watching parental examples. Children eventually throw their parents' negative attitudes back in their faces. Then the parents say, "How did that happen?" Children are an expression of parental character.

Home should be the place where we first experience forgiveness. If the home environment is forgiving and loving, we will always be willing to extend true forgiveness to others. Show me a home that knows how to restore people when they are in trouble, and that home will produce children who will also know how to restore others. One of the saddest indictments against many Christians today is their inability to forgive and restore people who make mistakes. Even Christian families teach their children to hold grudges and make judgments against those who fall by the wayside.

Unfortunately, the home is the first place we learn to gossip. Many people first hear negative comments about other people at the family dinner table. If a person is raised in a home where gossip is not allowed, that person will be reluctant to participate in gossip throughout his life. If anyone in my family ever made the mistake of saying something unkind about someone at our table, my father always stopped the conversation immediately. If we continued to gossip, we were chastised with the rod. My dad would say to us, "You don't know the circumstances. You have no right to make that judgment. If you can't say something good, don't say anything at all." I believe that principle should be taught in every home.

Children who exhibit poor manners in public places simply show that their parents do not require them to have good manners at home. A parent says, "Well, they know how they should behave because I have told them." Did that parent live out proper behavior in front of those children? If a child sees his dad elbowing everybody out of the way to get to the grits, gravy and cornbread, I promise the child will do the same thing. If Mom is always reaching for that last piece of chicken without making sure everyone else has a full plate, the children at the table are learning those same patterns. Parents will say, "Where did they learn that behavior?" They watched their parents. Children imitate what they see their parents do.

Finally, both good and bad concepts and attitudes toward sex are first learned by the way sex is regarded in the home. If little girls hear their mothers say that men are "animals," they will grow up believing that all men are abusive. A mother may tell her daughter, "All he wants is to get me into the bedroom." If we look closely at that woman's life, we discover a terrible mistake somewhere! A mother who has a negative attitude toward sex is not a sexually attractive role model for her daughter. I don't care if that mother has a figure like a Coca-Cola bottle, she is not sexually attractive. If a mother creates the thought in her little boy's mind that a woman expects to be sexually used and discarded, that attitude will affect his view of women all his life.

Parents who teach their children that sex is evil, wrong or risque produce adults who don't properly understand intimacy. What should a mother do if a little six-year-old boy wanders into her bedroom before she is dressed? Some women would scream in horror and the child would ask himself, "What have I done? What have I done?" He runs into the hall thinking, "That was a horrible thing I just did!" That child's confusion causes distorted attitudes about sex. I am not suggesting that family members go around exposing their bodies to little boys and girls, but we shouldn't make nudity seem like something evil or wrong. If by chance they walk into the room unexpectedly, a mother should be discrete in handling the situation. She should calmly tell the child that sometimes people need to have privacy.

The greatest compliment that can be paid to a parent is for a little boy or girl to ask that parent about sex. Unfortunately, most parents do not discuss sex openly. Children usually learn about sex from their friends or by watching an "R" rated movie on cable television. They grow up believing all sexuality is abusive, violent or self-gratifying, totally devoid of consideration or commitment. There is no easy way to say it. Too many parents don't have the guts to sit down and say to their children, "Sex is a gift from God. The decisions you make about this gift are very important."

A twelve-year-old son who has never discussed sex with his dad is likely to make horrible mistakes in his future relationships. That child will learn about sex somewhere. Some parents take a child to a barnyard to let him see two dogs or two cows mating. It just so happens that people are not dogs or cows! That strategy creates other problems as well. Too many people today are handling sex like dogs and cows. Children should be taught the value of their bodies' proper use as the temple of the Holy Spirit. They should know that their bodies are beautiful to God.

God observed His creation and said it was "good." The only reason man covered his body with leaves in the Garden of Eden was because he made such a mess of God's plan. Am I suggesting that when we finally move into the total restoration of mankind we won't wear any clothes? I don't know, but it sounds like a good idea to me. Some say that clothes "make people." Do they really? The point is that clothes are necessary because God could not trust us. I know that people who go to nudist colonies get into a mess, so please understand what I am saying. All the paraphernalia we wear is necessary because God cannot trust our choices. When we return to a totally proper relationship with God, limitations of this world will be eliminated.

Jesus said, "In the Kingdom, there is neither marriage nor giving in marriage." In the Kingdom we live at a higher dimension. Is marriage a lower dimension? Yes, it is. I am not suggesting "free love" at all. Please don't take these statements out of context. We must adhere to certain limitations in our lives because God cannot trust our decisions. Every limitation is necessary because God cannot trust us with freedom. Paul said of himself, "God trusts me at a level He cannot trust you." He said, "I have a right to eat any kind of meat I want, but I don't do certain things for your sakes. I know God and I abide by His character."

I am not suggesting any change in acceptable Christian lifestyles. I am saying that we are now living in limited relationships. Only when a man and his wife reach the maturity of a God-given, spiritually trusting relationship can they become an example of spiritual love to others. When we understand that goal, we understand how important it is that we project the proper sexual attitudes to boys and girls who follow our examples.

I can think of nothing more beautiful than a little child watching his father kiss his mother or hold her in his arms. Children love to see Mother playing with Dad by messing up his hair. Some husbands have their hair so stiff and starchy that if his wife touched it, it would scare him to death! Some women have the same problem. If anyone touched their hair, their heads would probably fall off. A man likes to feel a woman's head sometimes. Women go to bed with their hair rolled up in all those horrible curlers or wrapped in some kind of sack. A man never gets to touch a woman's head anymore. I can't understand why people want to destroy every good thing that God has made. We smother hair. We color it, redo it, overdo it and underdo it. God probably prefers for people to be natural-looking.

A "communication gap" is responsible for many problems in families. Family communication is often built around negative statements from one family member to another. Criticism and complaints are the beginning of many family conversations. A father sees his son's hair is getting too long and he says, "Well, I see your hair is still growing. When was the last time you got it cut? It looks filthy hanging down in your eyes."

Or perhaps a mother looks at her poor little daughter who wants to be approved and loved and says, "Well, who was that pimply-faced guy you went out with this time?" Those negative statements become our attempt at forming close relationships! Or we walk into a room and see a child reading a magazine and say, "Can't you find anything better to do? I'll put a broom in your hand so you can do something useful!"

The most damaging comments in families are made in situations when a man walks by his wife and pats her on some favorite part of her body that he likes to pat. She turns around and says, "You dog! Is that all you can think about?" Their poor children who are listening will never understand proper affections. At a party if somebody compliments a wife on how nice she looks in her party dress, all the way home in the car her husband accusingly asks her why that man was looking at her dress. Until then, her husband probably hadn't even bothered to look at her at all!

Wouldn't it be mind-boggling if a dad walked into a room where his son was break-dancing and said, "Son teach me how to do that"? The boy wouldn't know what to think! And then when that dad got down on the floor, he would absolutely cure his son from ever doing that dance again. Dad would look so strange, the kids would quit! Instead of that positive strategy, however, most parents go in saying, "My goodness! Is that all you can do?" If we start doing things with our children, we will build good relationships with them. Perhaps they will even stop break-dancing.

Boys finally began to cut their hair again a few years ago because their dads started growing long hair. In some cases, grandpas grew long hair, too. Youth want to have their own separate identities. They are trying to find an identity that belongs totally to them. They will grow long hair, plait their hair, grow odd-looking mustaches or do just about anything to have their own identities. They are really saying to their parents, "I am a human being, too."

What would happen to a teenage girl who had on tight pants if her mother walked up to her and said, "Let me try on your leather pants"? Instead mother usually says, "Good grief! Everyone can see every little bump." Put them on, Mom, and let her see how crazy they look. Some women put on their daughters' tight pants and liked them so much that they kept on wearing them. Now they look as ridiculous as their daughters do!

Young people are looking for ways to get attention. If they don't get attention for doing the right things, they will get attention in other ways. They want a daddy to sit down with them and say, "How is everything going? What do you need to share with me?" All kids want a close family.

Satan, the enemy, has tried to wreck the "close family" concept in America. First of all, Satan has almost eliminated family meals. He has manipulated kids through media bombardment to eat unhealthy junk foods and fast foods which have ruined traditional family dinners. Even when a mother serves good, nutritious foods, the family comes to the table saying, "I'm not hungry." Why? They've just finished eating chocolate chip cookies or a large bag of potato chips. Satan creates aberrations in appetites that have devastated family mealtimes that used to be a time for family fellowship.

When junk food doesn't separate the family, Satan disrupts family communication through television. Either the kids' favorite programs are on during dinner, or Dad wants to watch the news. Dad eats his dinner leaning over a television tray. His kid walks in saying, "Dad, I got an 'A' in school today." The father replies, "Will you shut up? The news is on." Twenty years later, that same kid will want to discuss something with someone, but he won't tell his dad. Dad is still too interested in the news. That child learned that the news was more important than he was.

I know children can take advantage of their parents.

I agree that children need to learn manners and consideration of their parents' time. If they are trained properly, they will know how to approach their parents to secure needed attention. When a parent is talking to someone and his child keeps interrupting, that parent needs to address the problem of training that child to be considerate.

God has given parents a major responsibility in teaching, training and living godly principles before their children. Parents need the help and covering of the church to reinforce spiritual values in the thinking and behavior of children from their earliest years. Together, the family and the church prepare "the seed" to grow strong and secure in the admonition of the Lord and in favor with God and man.

Without learning many wrong concepts, which many people of future generations must correct, the generation growing up under Kingdom teaching is prepared to live the witness which will challenge worldly concepts of sexuality. They will boldly address many rampant social problems by proclaiming, "It is written . . ." "God has said . . ." They will proclaim God's alternatives and solutions to a world seeking answers.

I pray for Christian homes to be like houses built on "the rock" which are not shaken in life's storms. I pray for spiritual fathers and mothers who will boldly prepare their children to influence society for good. Knowing truth, proclaiming truth and demonstrating truth in our daily lives are the greatest confrontations in our world today. As we follow the leading of the Holy Spirit, we are more than conquerors.

6

TURNED ON

Because I love young people and they know that I am honest with them, they feel free to ask me for answers to some of their most guarded questions. The adolescent period is a very confusing time of life. Identity struggles at any age are difficult, but adolescents are especially afraid of embarrassment or rejection in social situations. Young people often ask me to name the qualities in men or women which are attractive to the opposite sex. Unfortunately, I find that many adults are still searching for those same answers.

What really attracts a woman to a man? First, I want to address what does not turn on a woman. Big muscles do not turn her on. Guys spend large sums of money at the spa thinking their big muscles will attract the females. No, no, no! Most women would say big muscles actually look vulgar to them. Just ask a dozen girls if they like bulging biceps. Muscles don't impress girls —they impress other guys. Boys go to the spa with other boys. I'm not opposed to spas. I have a lifetime membership which was given to me. I haven't been in ten years, but I still have a lifetime membership!

The things men think impress women don't impress them. Guys with their shirts open down to their waists think they're really sexy. Their problem in thinking that is their egos—they are turned on by the mirror! Anybody walking into a restaurant with a shirt opened down to his waist ought to have his sanity questioned. That "macho" appearance does not turn on girls. "Mr. Macho" may turn on a twelve or thirteen-year-old girl who does not know any better, but when she matures, she will laugh at him, too.

Women are not impressed with men who try a lot of different hair styles. I think some men try to see how many hair styles they can create in a month. If they can't blow it dry in some wild style, they will put grease on it. If they can't grease it down, they will part it differently. Men are really more vain than women. Women are naturally fickle and should be allowed to try various styles. But variety in a man's appearance is not really attractive to a woman.

Men think a woman is turned on if he has a cigarette hanging out of his mouth. Crude behavior is no turn-on. Bad habits really make a woman sick.

What turns on a guy? Let us first say what does not turn him on. Women's crazy clothes do not turn on men.

She can put her waistline under her arm or down to her knees, and most men couldn't care less. Women are only impressing other women and sometimes effeminate men. The latest styles do not turn on guys. Although women won't admit it, many fashion designers have lifestyles which they abhor. These same women wear those designers' clothes. Many fashionable clothes don't even reveal whether they are made to be worn by a man or a woman. We allow people who are not well-adjusted individuals to control current clothing styles. Paul said, "Be not conformed to their traditions."

I plead with talented Christian designers to create good, attractive styles. Women's styles should be very feminine. Men need to look like men because the Bible says that it is shameful for a man to look like a woman (Deuteronomy 22:5). Equally appalling is a woman who tries to look like a man. The idea of everyone trying to look the same is just not God's design in creation with such variety of shapes and colors. A girl's clothes should complement her body. No single style will ever do that. No single hem length is proper for all women. We need to learn to dress in order to complement the physique God gave us. God did not make us stupid. We turn people off sometimes when we think we are turning them on.

Long eyelashes don't turn men on; they only get in their way. A man doesn't like a woman to leave smudges all over his face. Men don't like long fingernails. I have never known a man in my life who did. Long fingernails impress other women with the fact that a woman never washes dishes. She also doesn't change diapers because she would claw the baby to death if she did. She can't even open doors or comb her hair. Those things are not going to turn on a man. Men will put up with trends out of love for women, but the latest trends don't turn them on. Tight jeans don't turn men on either. Women think they look sexy, but they don't. Men know those jeans are uncomfortable. They say, "Poor thing! Look how she walks. She can hardly make it."

No one can surprise me about human relationships after what I have heard in counseling through forty years of ministry. Some stories I've heard are so wild that they would be improper to share!

A woman is turned on by a man who cares. She is attracted to a man who is not self-centered. She wants a man who does not believe the whole world is created for his own personal service and convenience. A woman wants someone who is mannerly, but not excessively so. She wants consideration in good manners, but not so much formality that she will become uncomfortable. A man's manners ought to be so second nature to him that a woman doesn't even notice his efforts. A woman wants to be a part of a man in a caring way. Good manners support and enhance that desire.

One of the saddest requests I ever hear is whenever a young man says to me, "Pastor, I don't really know how to behave with a girl whom I want to impress. I never saw my father do anything mannerly for my mother. I don't even know what you mean when you talk about the way a gentleman behaves with a lady."

Sometimes a man helps a woman out of a car in a way that makes her very uncomfortable. A woman is awkward in a certain length dress when she gets out of a car. If a man doesn't know how to help her, she would rather he not assist her at all. These are just basic courtesies that men rarely think about these days. Many men are too eager to jump out of the car and run to the hamburger stand. The poor woman comes dragging along twelve feet behind him.

A woman is attracted to consistency and dependability in a man. If one day he treats her like she is worthless and the next day she is God's gift to him, what does the woman have to depend upon? She never knows which mood will hit him the next time they are together. Everything in her life depends upon his varying moods. She says, "I'll have to see what kind of mood he is in." If that statement ever refers to a Christian man, his relationship is in trouble. A man should not have the privilege of unpredictable moods. Perhaps a woman does occasionally, but in certain areas, men should always be consistent.

If a man ever gets so angry with his wife that he cannot pray with her before they go to sleep, he is not spiritually consistent. Some of the most corrective times in my life have come at the close of the day. When I was a young preacher, I felt so pressured and guilty after any conflict with my wife, Norma, that I would say to her, "Let's pray." Then I would pray in her presence, "God, I have not been a good husband today. I really wouldn't want my people to know what a poor husband I have been." I would feel her arms slip around me, knowing she had heard my spirit, and she would say, "It's all right, Earl, I love you." Families don't have to fall apart. Couples need to listen closely to the Spirit of God in each other.

What turns on a man? Perhaps I am more qualified to answer this question than to speak for the feminine mind. I am going to surprise many women when I say that a man is not necessarily attracted by a woman's good looks. Notice how sometimes the most popular girls are some of the most homely and unattractive. Why? Boys can identify with an imperfect girl. Some girls become "wallflowers" because they are too pretty to touch. There is nothing wrong with beauty, but a woman should keep it simple.

When I was in college, I saw a beautiful girl watching us boys play football one afternoon. I turned to someone and asked, "Do you know who that girl is? I'd like to get to know her."

One of my friends said to me, "You can't date her because her mother doesn't allow her to go out with anyone." She had won the Miss Parker contest, and later she became Miss Furman, then Miss South Carolina, and finally first-runner-up to Miss America.

I walked over to her and said "Hi, I'm Earl."

She said, "I know who you are. My aunt's singing group sings sometimes at your dad's church."

"I would like to see you Saturday," I said.

She said, "OK, but I don't know how my mom will react to that invitation."

"Let me deal with your mother," I told her.

Saturday, when I walked into her house, I said, "Hey, Mother, where are you?"

She said, "I'm in the kitchen washing dishes."

I walked into the kitchen, grabbed a towel and asked, "Do you need any help?" After I'd made all the points I needed to make, I said to her mother, "I would like to take Esther for a ride. Is that all right with you?"

She said, "That will be great!" Esther almost fainted. For the first time, her mother trusted a young man. The point is that some women are too pretty. Esther was one of the most beautiful women I have ever seen. She was so pretty that boys were afraid of her. A lot of women do not understand that too much beauty is a threat to many men.

If a girl is not having many dates, she needs to pull her hair down in her face, take off some of her makeup and walk a little differently. Maybe then the boys will not be afraid to speak to her. Extreme, unattainable beauty does not attract men. That doesn't mean a man does not want a woman to look pretty. Femininity will always turn him on. Sometimes simply the way a woman moves or reaches out to people will attract him. A man wants a touchable woman. I am not saying that every woman needs to be touched by strange men. A touchable woman is one who is not a fixture or a "prima donna" to such a degree that she can't be reached.

A woman is most attractive whenever she is comforting to a man. A man needs a woman who can comfort him. If she is more worried about messing up her hair than a man's feelings, he may look at her, but she will never meet his needs.

A man is turned on by a woman who knows how to be pursued. If the woman is the one who does the chasing, she makes a tragic mistake. She may even get a man into the bedroom, but he will never make the considerate, caring husband she really wants. A man has an innate desire within him to pursue a woman. A lady says, "I have been waiting for four years to be pursued." The problem may have to do with a negative attitude. Also some women are pursued and don't even recognize it.

A man wants a true friend, someone he can talk with freely. He is looking for someone who is not so self-centered that she expects to be told she is beautiful the first time they talk together. When a couple can talk about school or their interests and goals, a relationship can be established on a firm foundation. An approachable woman who really understands a man will attract him.

What turns on a man? A woman who is resilient and not easily broken, who doesn't run and cry over every little problem, who is not fixed in her thoughts or too opinionated. Men do not like opinionated women. Men like women to have convictions, but not unbendable opinions. An opinionated woman has controlling spirits.

Esther in the Old Testament is the classic example of the woman a man would pursue. In the same story, Queen Vashti is an example of an opinionated woman. Esther walked into the king's presence, knowing she could get anything she wanted, but also knowing how to approach the king humbly. She waited until the scepter was extended to her. The whole kingdom was hers because she knew how to move with authority. A fine line of humility distinguishes the difference between controlling spirits and spiritual conviction.

I don't always totally agree with Jerry Falwell. We are alike in many areas of ministry, but we are also very different in other areas. One thing that I do admire about Jerry Falwell is that he is a man of conviction who believes whatever he says. I will give a man a lot of rope if he has strong convictions.

I have prayed above all things that people in my congregation would become people of conviction. The most attractive women in the world are ones who have strong convictions. The Lord said to a particular woman in my congregation recently, "Tell your friend who is married to one of a different faith that the only way that friend can survive spiritually is to receive the baptism of the Holy Spirit." It took conviction and courage to say that to this particular individual. The friend started arguing, but the fact is that conviction had its way. Women who compromise will be used as rags and will eventually be thrown away. Attractive women have convictions, but they are not opinionated.

Three things will kill a relationship. The first way to kill intimacy is by "smothering" love. Truth sets us free; it does not smother us. A relationship can never be maintained because someone demands attention. A relationship is sealed in trust. Even when an individual is wrong about something, a relationship will continue if trust is maintained.

The second way to kill a relationship is public embarrassment. If a husband or a wife announces their bedroom problems in public, that mate will be so turned off that the chances of recovery in that marriage are almost impossible. A wife begins to fear that if she becomes vulnerable, the whole world will know her problems by the way her husband treats her publicly. During my forty years in ministry, I've seen numerous examples of men who abused their wives publicly. Many wives have been just as cruel. Once I heard a woman call her husband "a garbage mouth." I watched him die on the spot. Her life later unfolded in devastation and destruction while her marriage ended in a divorce. What am I saying? I am saying, "Don't embarrass your partner. Covering problems publicly builds trust in private intimacy."

The Bible says that love covers. If a wife is as cold as a refrigerator, don't publicly tell everyone that she is "an ice cube." Maybe a husband is going through a time of mental problems, but a wife should not publicly expose his impotence. She should be his covering.

The third way to kill a relationship is by a lack of maturity. When a woman gets married, she does not want a husband who acts like a little boy. When a man marries, he doesn't want a little girl who "runs home to Mommy" whenever she gets upset. Too many people never separate from "Mommy." They even look for a partner whose personality helps them maintain that dominant parental relationship.

Wrong decisions will kill relationships. Establishing criteria by which a couple make decisions is critical. I speak out of my experience but also by example. Many relationships surround my life at various dimensions. I can say without any reservations that my wife and I have remained firm in our covenant commitment even through difficult times. She has never once threatened to leave me. I have never once said to her, "I am going home to Momma."

The truth is that sex is God's idea not only as a plan of procreation, but also as a plan of restoration and recreation. Intimate togetherness knits a couple together. Sex has far more meaning than just the physical process of having children. Sex makes two become one when it is proper and right. A couple know each other because they say who they really are in those unguarded moments. Intimacy can also bring us to a high dimension of prayer. In unguarded moments when our walls are down, we say to God, "Here I am, God." In those moments of spiritual intimacy, a person's life can be changed. If we go to our companions with our fences and walls up, they will never know us as we really are.

A mature relationship is one in which two adults under God honestly know who they are. They can be open to one another without being afraid. Intimacy is not "consenting adults doing whatever they want." True intimacy is two spiritually mature people who complement one another to such a degree that everything they do pleases God. For that reason I say repeatedly, "The Kingdom waits for an example."

7

TRUE FULFILLMENT

Language that relates to sexuality is used boldly in pornographic books, back alleys and offensive jokes. Sexuality is seldom confronted as a reality of every person's life, especially by the Church. Because of extreme attitudes of exploitation or suppression, our society flourishes with perversions, aberrations and false information on the subject of sex. Many boys and girls grow up thinking that something is unusual and even sinful about their sexuality.

Let your fountain be blessed, and rejoice with the wife of your youth. As a loving deer and a graceful doe, let her breasts satisfy you at all times; and always be enraptured with her love. For why should you, my son, be enraptured by an immoral wom-

an, and be embraced in the arms of a seductress? (Proverbs 5:18-20)

This scripture contains many of the secrets of an ongoing, successful sexual relationship. "Fountain" in verse eight does not refer to water; it refers to sex. These verses refer to relationships. "As a loving deer and a graceful doe . . ." That description should give insight to women on ways to be attractive. Nothing attracts a man to a deliberately masculine woman. A woman who thinks feminine thoughts will have feminine movements. Many people think that the only purpose of the breasts is to nurse babies. Only an unlearned sexual partner could believe that.

Nothing is more satisfying to a man and a woman than fulfilling the needs they have for physically touching. Physical touching, apart from the sexual act, is emotionally satisfying to human beings. Unfortunately, too many times men never even pause to recognize the gift that God has given in the body of a woman. Too often men only quickly satisfy and gratify themselves.

How fair is your love, my sister, my spouse! How much better than wine is your love, and the scent of your perfumes than all spices! Your lips, O my spouse, drip as the honeycomb; honey and milk are under your tongue; and the fragrance of your garments is like the fragrance of Lebanon. A garden enclosed is my sister, my spouse, a spring shut up, a fountain sealed. (Song of Solomon 4:10-12)

Unfortunately, we usually think of perfume as something we buy at a department store. Exotic perfume is not the reference in these verses. A basic scent of love is acceptable to men, yet it frightens most women. Understand that sometimes a bath is more important to a man than all the commercial perfumes a woman could pour on her body! A woman whose presence is smelled before she is seen will not be more attractive because of her fragrance. God made no mistakes in preparing our bodies to function. Until we understand God's purposes in creation, we will spend a lifetime buying expensive things to help us be more attractive that are almost meaningless and worthless. (I do not suggest that we stop using deodorant. As a matter of fact, I suggest that we do.)

Fastidious people are never good lovers. They don't comprehend what vulnerability is all about. They concentrate too much on seeing that their hair doesn't get messed up. They respond to affection by saying, "Don't smudge my make-up."

"A spring shut up, a fountain sealed . . ." Jesus picked up on this verse when He said, "Out of your belly shall flow rivers of living water." Why did He say "belly"? Why didn't He say "arm" or "leg"? Jesus knew that the source of life is the womb, the stomach, or as the New King James interprets it, "the heart." Lifted to a spiritual dimension, life flows from our innermost beings in proper relationships. Unfortunately, the Church has never quite comprehended that principle. If we are to be the generation who will usher in the Kingdom of God in full measure, I believe we must first begin to comprehend spiritual relationships.

Jesus gave us direction in bringing the Kingdom to earth when He said, "Two basic relationships fulfill all the Law and the Prophets." Jesus said that we are to love God with all our hearts, and our neighbors as ourselves. Because we are not willing to obey His commandments, we spend our time perverting good things of God and letting the devil have our affections. The same devil who motivates the belly dancers to entertain the world will laugh when I declare that out of the belly flow resources and life. Once we comprehend relationships properly, we can find sustenance in them.

The woman at the well is symbolic of the Church today that needs to discover a new source. Jesus was not just dealing with a woman, He was dealing with the Church that needs fulfillment. Think of her as the Church and not as a woman when she said, "Give me something that will cause me never to thirst again. Give me this internalized water that will bubble up inside of me." Jesus said, "I can give you that water, but first call your husband."

Apart from right relationships, we can never receive the fulfillment of God. The Church will be thirsty until it discovers its proper structure and headship. When the Church is finally fulfilled, she will return to the marketplaces saying, "Come, see the Messiah! The Kingdom is here!"

The Church today desperately needs fulfillment and satisfaction. People run everywhere looking for natural waters to bring satisfaction when refreshing living waters will flow freely only from a right relationship with God. Because the Church has been ignored and regarded as either a weak authority or no authority at all, headship is meaningless to the world and even to many Christians. God tells the Church today, "Call your husband." Most people don't even know where and when to call an elder.

Moreover, brethren, I do not want you to be unaware that all our fathers were under the cloud, all passed through the sea, all were baptized into Moses in the cloud and in the sea, all ate the same spiritual food, and all drank the same spiritual drink. For they drank of that spiritual Rock that followed them, and that Rock was Christ. But with most of them God was not well pleased, for their bodies were scattered in the wilderness. Now these things became our examples, to the intent that we should not lust after evil things as they also lusted. And do not become idolaters as were some of them. As it is written, "The people sat down to eat and drink, and rose up to play." Nor let us commit sexual immorality, as some of them did, and in one day twenty-three thousand fell; nor let us tempt Christ, as some of them also tempted, and were destroyed by serpents; nor murmur, as some of them also murmured, and were destroyed by the destroyer. Now all these things happened to them as examples, and they were written for our admonition, on whom the ends of the ages have come. (I Corinthians 10:1-11)

The Israelites drank water that came out of a rock. That rock was a symbol of Christ. If Christ is exemplified by water which springs from the rock, then we as Christians who are filled with the Holy Spirit are symbolized by springs of water which flow from within us. The spiritual flow is a life-giving virtue.

The Church in the wilderness (Israel) should exemplify for us the reasons we are not entering into fulfillment of God's promises. Notice, five reasons listed:

First of all, lust is Satan's tool for destroying God-given sexuality. Lust is self-gratification, a "taker" mentality. Lust comes from the kingdom of darkness. Lust cannot even function or exist in the Kingdom of Light. If an individual is motivated by lust, that area of

SEX IS GOD'S IDEA

his life has never entered the Kingdom. Many people have continuous, insoluble, relationship problems for that very reason. Love gives, but lust takes. Lust steals and destroys virtue. Lust asks for something but gives nothing in return. Lust does not care if a companion is content or satisfied. Lust demands, but love requests. Love is giving and always desires the best interest of someone else.

The Apostle Paul said that when we enter into a covenant relationship, we are no longer the ones in control of our lives. Our desires are to fulfill our companions. Self-centered desires are not motivated by the Holy Spirit. Christians must enter relationships saying, "What can I give?" instead of "What am I going to get out of this?" Even if we have had the Holy Spirit for forty years, if we enter into relationships based on what we can get, we are still operating by lust. Lust keeps us from receiving the promises of God. This teaching is right at the heart of Kingdom theology. Lust will prevent Christians from achieving the maturity that will allow the Kingdom to come.

Satan's second tool is idolatry. Idolatry in the wilderness finally resulted in Israel's worshiping the golden calf. Idolatry always results in religious perversion. Idolatry misdirects priorities. What are our priorities? What are the most important desires in our lives? Is our basic concern for the family or for something else? Idolatry does not mean worshiping some little statue sitting on the mantle. Idolatry is that which dominates our interests. We must commit our hearts to "having a date" with God when it is time for the church to assemble. Paul said that in the last days, people would no longer desire to go to God's house.

That attitude is a result of idolatry or misdirected priorities.

The third tool of Satan is fornication. Fornication deals with spiritual mixture and is not the same as adultery. Jezebel, a woman in the church of Thyatira described in the book of Revelation, symbolized fornication because she led the people into deception (Revelation 2:20). The cause of God is hindered more by the act of fornication in the Spirit than by a sinful, sexual act of the flesh. Fornication is a spiritual sin, while adultery is a flesh sin.

It is interesting to note that people can commit spiritual fornication yet never be asked to leave the church. However, if someone in that same church committed adultery—by comparison, a far less damaging act of the flesh—all hell would literally break loose. Deceivers and those who create mixture among God's people in a congregation are left unchallenged although they can totally destroy faith. Their deceptive tactics can eventually lead people who do not have a strong spiritual foundation to hell. Mixture, refusing truth and being swayed by the opinions of others are examples of spiritual fornication.

Tempting Christ is Satan's fourth tool. Satan said to Jesus, "If You are the son of God, throw Yourself down." Jesus refused Satan's tests because compliance would have been following the will of Satan. If God had said the same thing to Jesus, He would have done it. Two people can do exactly the same thing, yet one tempts God and the other pleases God. One person could give an offering of a hundred dollars out of obedience, and his motivation would please God. Another person could give the same amount to be seen or to try

SEX IS GOD'S IDEA

to buy a place of authority, and that offering would be tempting God.

If we pray in opposition to God's character and will, we are tempting Him. If we ask God for something we shouldn't have, James says that our requests are lustful. Lustful desires gratify our own flesh and do not honor God.

The fifth tool of Satan is murmuring. If ever a sin has yet to be dealt with positively, that sin is murmuring. Until murmuring among God's people is conquered, we will never become the prototype to the world that God has called us to be. One person may ask an honest question to find direction, but another person may ask questions as a way to murmur and complain. God despised no sin of the Israelites in the wilderness more than murmuring. Murmuring lowers one's self-image and destroys character.

A husband or wife who embarrasses each other in public places probably commits an unpardonable mistake in a marital relationship. To cause a husband or wife to feel embarrassed is to embarrass Christ. If we understand that truth in marriage, we will save ourselves much heartache. Sometimes criticism is made by innuendo, a shrug of a shoulder, or snapping back with sharp remarks. The Kingdom of God waits for people who do not murmur and complain.

Four things in our relationships keep us from Kingdom fulfillment. First, we will be unfulfilled in relationships until we understand the proper role of a male and female. A man and a woman in total obedience to God create headship. If we violate the role that God chooses for us, we totally cut off the flow of His power in our lives. The roles of a husband and wife in a covenant relationship under God absolutely complement one another.

A woman is likely to be given to details. She does not mind collecting specific items on a shopping list. People who surround me know that details drive me crazy, and that is probably true of most men. Men really don't want to know the specific details of issues. They would rather have a general appraisal of a situation. They want to know basic facts about what is taking place here and there. They want to know the headlines of the news. Probably the only detail a man cares about knowing is the score of a football game!

Women are emotional. A woman could not be a discerner if she were not innately emotional. She has a right to cry easily. When men cry easily, they are either experiencing spiritual dealings of God or are in the midst of a nervous breakdown. That is not the case with a woman. Crying is her release. A woman is the emotional release to a man. A woman is also suspicious by nature. Her curiosity makes her a good discerner if she knows how to lift that characteristic to a spiritual dimension. God can give women discernment if they do not content themselves with simply being suspicious instead of discerning the truth. A woman is very sensitive. If a husband does not tap her sensitivity, she will never respond to him.

A man generalizes. A man who is able to tell someone what color tie every other man wore to church on Sunday is very rare. But a woman will say, "Did you notice those purple and grey and orange shoes that Mary had on? Did you notice that Sally has changed her hairdo?" A man sits there in a daze. He does not notice these things. Men are not given to noting details.

A man has a calculating mind regarding business pursuits. By nature he has a way of calculating certain things that might be totally unfamiliar territory to a woman. These characteristics are always dimensional within us. We are all male and female. All of us have both male and female hormones. Balance determines which one dominates.

Female characteristics make a person more suspicious, more jealous or more controlling. A female always wants more details. If a man feeds the masculine characteristics that are normal for his role, details will not be nearly so important. He will understand how to generalize information without getting lost in details. If a man scrapes his finger over the top of every door in the house to see if his wife has dusted, he is a man of details. If he looks under the bed every day to see whether his wife has cleaned, he is too preoccupied with details.

A man also needs assistance in releasing his emotions. A woman will inevitably release her emotions. Sometimes she may keep them locked away for awhile, but one way or another, she will release them. If she can't express herself openly, she will wait until everyone goes to work or school, and she will go to the bedroom to cry. If a man does that, call for the padded wagon. He is in trouble. Instead, most men will sit in a chair and pout over their problems. Men do not know how to release their emotions. A woman must learn how to help him find a way to release them.

The second hindrance to Kingdom fulfillment in relationships comes from failing to understand headship. We must come to an understanding of what we mean by "rule" and "servanthood." Paul asked how a man could rule in God's Church when he could not rule his own family. Substitute the word "serve" for the word "rule." How can a man serve in God's house when he cannot serve his own family? Service points to the requirements of an elder and deacon. The Lord has given specific requirements related to the household of a leader in the Church. His wife must be in subjection, temperate and not a gossiper. A leader must have his house in order and his children under control.

One of the grave problems in God's Church comes about when people try to be leaders without having their own houses in order. Some people say that they don't have time for their families. They will have time in eternity to stand before God and be judged for neglecting their households. When I talk about rulership, I talk about service.

People are qualified to rule according to the level of their ability to serve or to minister. God will give someone responsibility for the number of people for which that person is able to be responsible. God designates authority according to one's ability to serve. In worldly terms, we talk about lordship over somebody. As Christians, we talk about the greatest among us being the one who will serve the most people. If a pastor is what he should be, his life is given to service—never to lordship.

Until we understand servanthood, the Kingdom cannot become a reality in total manifestation. A man who knows how to serve his own family and is respected by them because he knows how to minister to them will also be able to minister to the household of faith. For that reason, the Bible says that before we select someone to rule in God's house, that person must first be proven. How is someone proven? First in his personal life, and then in circumstances at lower dimensions of responsibility in ministry.

How does a man minister to his wife? He ministers to her by understanding her. A wife needs understanding from her husband when he comes home at the end of the day. If she has been at home all day with the children she is tired. Minister to her by not coming in saying, "Why are you late with dinner? Why is your hair in your eyes?" Instead say, "Honey, let me help you get things together." A husband needs to move in ministry and service in his home. He puts things in order for his wife and thereby ministers to her.

A wife wants her husband to understand when she is tired. He needs to think of ways in which he can refresh her. Let's start with a hot bath with heated towels and a good rub down with lotion. A man asks, "If I do that for her, then what will she do for me?" You nut! Don't be so obvious!

A woman receives ministry when a man simply listens to her. He doesn't always have to be reading the newspaper or listening to the news. Nearby sits a little woman who wants someone to listen to her. Someone will listen to her eventually and she is going to respond to that person. A husband then says, "How did it happen? Look at all of these muscles I have built by weightlifting." Some plain little guy who may be nothing special to look at will walk away with his arm around her. Why? He listened to her. A brokenhearted husband can kick dust in the little guy's eyes, but sensitivity has won the woman's heart. That is the reason that sometimes a man's best friend will marry his wife. That best friend listened to her.

How does a man minister to a woman? He respects her opinions and lets her make observations. When she says something, he doesn't say, "You don't know anything about that." I know a woman who decided to learn a few football-related phrases. She thought she could interject them whenever the men were talking. The men would be sitting around talking about football and she would say, "Maybe they ought to red dog." If her husband were smart, when she interjected a little phrase, he would say, "That's great." If she were completely dumb about football, he should still accept what she says in a positive way.

Someone says, "That's patronization." No, that approval is understanding that a woman wants to be involved. To minister to a woman is to respect what she says. I am bothered to see separation of men and women taking place at many parties. Men go in one room to talk and the women go in another. I am also not impressed with the concept of all-boys' or all-girls' schools. How will young people in an exclusive environment ever learn to live in a world that is real?

How does a woman minister to a man? First, she must believe in him. She needs to believe that he is an authority in his field. If she does not believe in him, he will never have a positive image of himself. The wife may say, "I only believe what this great authority says." Instead, she needs to start believing the words of her husband! A woman needs to find areas where she regards her husband as totally believable. Neither a man nor the relationship will ever develop properly until a wife believes in her husband.

How does a woman minister to a man? Sometimes she needs to comfort him as she would a little boy. Oddly enough, there is a lot of little boy left in a man. Sometimes he just wants to be touched. If a man reacts adversely to his wife running her fingers through his hair, he is probably a hopeless case. If a man's coiffure will not allow a little roughhousing, he had better change it. One of the finest ways a man can be comforted is for his wife to stand behind him and run her fingers through his hair. I know that sounds so trite, but it is the truth.

Recently, a woman told me, "I really wanted to minister to my husband when he came home after work, but if I even touched his hair, he would slap my hand. He even wrote his name on his comb." That kind of man cannot receive comfort. A good lover learns to be touchable.

A woman can minister to a man by helping him change his pace, by learning how to get him out of a rut. If someone doesn't relieve his pressures, they will become a grave to him. If he sets his mind too much in one direction, move it into another area of interest. If his wife doesn't help to change her husband's pace, chances are he will get out of balance. The wife is the one to give his life variety. Have something planned that is enticing to him. Even if a trip to his mother-in-law's house is planned, make him anticipate that he is going to a great place to have a great time. Get his mind going in some other direction. That suggestion may sound insignificant, but it can make a great difference in a man's life.

The third hindrance to Kingdom fulfillment in relationships is that the Body has not been redeemed. "The whole earth groans waiting for the manifestation of the sons of God" (Romans 8:19). This passage goes on to say that the Body is not yet redeemed (verse 23). I have always heard that passage interpreted to mean that our bodies have not overcome the law of sin and death. I'm sure that is not an improper interpretation because the body is indeed in the process of redemption. But if we read with spiritual understanding, we will see that Paul said something totally different from what we may have thought.

For I consider that the sufferings of this present time are not worthy to be compared with the glory which shall be revealed in us. For the earnest expectation of the creation eagerly waits for the revealing of the sons of God. For the creation was subjected to futility, not willingly, but because of Him who subjected it in hope; because the creation itself also will be delivered from the bondage of corruption into the glorious liberty of the children of God. For we know that the whole creation groans and labors with birth pangs together until now. And not only they, but we also who have the firstfruits of the Spirit, even we ourselves groan within ourselves, eagerly waiting for the adoption, the redemption of our body. (Romans 8:18-23)

Unfortunately, the Body has not been redeemed. When the Body is redeemed, its proper structure of the apostle, prophet, pastor, teacher and evangelist will flow in their ministries. The gifts of the Spirit will operate to edify the Body. The fruit of the Spirit will be flowing in believers. Then the full redemption of the body of Christ is fulfilled. Then and only then can Christ return.

Ministry in the Body is blocked because the Body is not redeemed and relationships are out of order.

149

Someone says, "I need scripture for that!"

Likewise you wives, be submissive to your own husbands, that even if some do not obey the word, they, without a word, may be won by the conduct of their wives, when they observe your chaste conduct accompanied by fear. Do not let your beauty be that outward adorning of arranging the hair, of wearing gold, or of putting on fine apparel; but let it be the hidden person of the heart, with the incorruptible ornament of a gentle and quiet spirit, which is very precious in the sight of God. For in this manner, in former times, the holy women who trusted in God also adorned themselves, being submissive to their own husbands, as Sarah obeyed Abraham, calling him lord whose daughters you are if you do good and are not afraid with any terror. (I Peter 3:1-6)

Wives who divorce their husbands only because their conduct is improper do not understand God's Word. There are justifiable reasons to leave a marriage, but those reasons are not the ones most people consider to be "good" reasons.

Adultery is not necessarily a reason for divorce. God's Word says that only "fornication" justifies divorce in the marriages of Christian people. Fornication is a spiritual sin—adultery is a sin of the flesh. A partner who has committed the sin of fornication has walked away from God, willfully recognizing all the consequences of that choice. Sometimes flesh sins provoke spiritual fornication, but only spiritual authority in the local church can judge in this matter. A person unwilling to submit to spiritual authority is out of God's will in seeking a divorce. Few Christian couples would ever divorce if they both submitted their problems to the authority of the church.

The wise man in Proverbs wrote about a beautiful woman whose price was far above rubies (Proverbs 31). She so cares for her household that when winter comes, she is not afraid because she kept the candle burning all night to prepare covering for her household. The writer is not talking about household responsibilities. He is talking about the preparation and readiness of this woman's spirit. A man's security rests in a godly woman.

Likewise you husbands, dwell with them with understanding, giving honor to the wife, as to the weaker vessel, and as being heirs together of the grace of life, that your prayers may not be hindered. (I Peter 3:7)

Improper relationships definitely hinder our spirituality. If the man of the household is not spiritually minded, God must circumvent him. The thrust of the church should be to raise up men who are spiritual leaders in their own households. These men will call a pastor on the authority of God whenever necessary. That pastor can confidently say to a husband, "Anoint your wife with oil, and she will be made well." A spiritually mature husband would so believe the Word of God that when he anointed his wife in accordance with pastoral direction, she would be healed. That household demonstrates proper order. Children unquestionably respect a loving, spiritual father as the head of the house.

". . . that your prayers be not hindered." Is Peter talking about the household of faith? In the second chapter of I Peter he talks about the "chosen generation" and "lively stones." Peter is talking about this generation when he says that our relationships keep the Kingdom from being established. If a man cannot rule in his house as a priest to his own wife and children, he is disregarding God's calling for his life. Many of the same men who come into God's house wanting to be rulers and leaders serve only to prostitute true spiritual authority.

I have come to believe that lack of obeying civil law is also a hindrance to answered prayers. This may seem bold, but I believe if we fail to observe the traffic safety laws that civil authority demands, God will not respect the law of prayer in our lives.

I believe that God has arranged a definite set of circumstances to establish His authority in creation. God's established line of command is authority flowing directly from the hand of God through Christ, the Head of the Church, to the Church on the earth. Authority flows from the Church to the husband and then to the wife in Christian families. When we follow that structure, we receive the same answer to our prayers that Jesus gave to the centurion concerning his remarkable faith. The centurion told Jesus, "Jesus, I am a man under authority, and I understand Your command is all that is needed to heal my servant." A lack of understanding rightful authority in God's Church today is the major reason that God's miracles are not more evident.

I know that God is speaking a strong message today. I also know confirmations will come from many spiritual voices that carnal relationships hinder Kingdom manifestation. The Bible says, "Fathers, don't provoke your children." "Children, learn obedience under your parents as faith in the Lord." God is trying to teach us how to respond to His authority in one another. God's authority comes to us through human authority which is led by the Holy Spirit. We cannot respond to God's authority until we respond to human authority in God's designated order.

Anyone who prevents a spiritual father from managing the affairs of his children is circumventing the laws of God. God's flow in authority is cut off from those children. What if that father is not a spiritual man? He still has the right to control that household in all natural matters and decisions. He cannot rule in spiritual decisions, such as whether or not his children can go to church. However, in natural areas such as the kind of car the family will drive, he has the right and responsibility to lead the family. But he cannot keep his family from praying. He cannot keep his family from following God in spiritual obedience. If a family follows God's Word carefully, their witness will often cause a father eventually to believe in God's authority.

How long is a child under the authority of a household? As long as he lives in that household, he is under its authority. Jesus was subject to his parents until He was thirty years old. At twelve, He went home with his parents from the temple, and the Bible says that He was subject to them. If a thirty-year-old son lives with his parents, the father still remains the head of that household. When women learn to support their husbands' decisions, homes will be set in proper order and will reflect the order in God's house. Problems with authority in the Church would never exist if authority were understood in individual homes.

The fourth hindrance to fulfilled Kingdom relationships is a generation in bondage. Jesus said, "You shall know the truth, and truth will set you free" (John 8:32).

Until the Church establishes God's order, we delay the establishment of God's Kingdom on earth. A freed generation is one that does not react negatively to truth. A freed generation can talk about sex with mature understanding. A freed generation is not too intimidated to talk about things like menopause, masturbation, or sexual satisfaction through what we call "a climax," which may be a totally erroneous understanding of sexual satisfaction for a woman.

For the male ego, a physical response is his only assurance that he has accomplished some great erotic goal. Few men realize that the experience might not minister to a woman at all. If that is not understood in God's house among God's people who are free to discuss any problem, how will we ever become an example in every area of life to the world?

I have been openly bold with the youth in my church. We have exceptionally mature young people in my congregation who understand far more at their ages than most of my generation did. I am willing to answer their questions honestly. Some of them had been told that they were "going blind" because they involved themselves in self-manipulation. A confused generation is misinformed because Christian parents are not willing to engage in responsible dialogue and moral training with their children. The subject of sex is all "hush-hush." There is a place for people to be thankful to God for all aspects of their bodies.

I once counseled a man who had been married twenty-eight years. He said, "I have never seen my wife's body totally nude." That degree of modesty is not emotionally healthy. Yet physical overexposure in the marriage relationship can violate the need for privacy

154

just as much. Overexposure is just not that attractive. Sexual maturity conveys to a lover the way to be attractive.

A lot of women think that when they go through menopause, they will lose their sexual desires. Studies prove that menopause has absolutely nothing to do with sexual desires. After a woman goes through menopause, she may be far more relaxed in a sexual relationship than ever before because the fear of pregnancy is eliminated.

How did David's court determine that the king was dying? They brought a young beautiful woman and put her at his feet. When he did not respond, they knew David's time was running out. Many people give up on life long before they should.

Some people lose their sexuality because they do not take care of their bodies. Physical obstructions—a beard, excess weight, bad breath or body odor—may prohibit enjoyment of sexual activities. If a person cares for himself as long as he lives, sex should continue to be a normal part of life. Sexual activity may change in desire, dimension or frequency, but intimacy should continue until death. Sex is not something about which we say, "When I was a child, I thought like a child. I went to bed like a child. But when I became mature, I put away childish things." No! That person put away an important gift that God gave him to maintain an intimate relationship.

God has given us sex for far more than just the creation of babies. Sex is also given to people for recreation. It is a resource, a way to take our minds away from harsh realities of daily life. The experience surrounds us and brings us into a human relationship that yields warmth, understanding and acceptance. No act of acceptance is greater than sexual expression in a God-given covenant relationship between a husband and wife. Sex is intended not only for recreation and procreation, but also as a way of communication whose intimacy brings close understanding.

I want to share this prayer written by Harry Hollis, Jr.

"Lord, it is difficult to know what sex really is. Is it some demon sent to torment me or some delicious seducer from reality? It is neither of these, Lord, I know what sex is. It is body and Spirit. It is passion and tenderness. It is strong embraces and gentle hand-holding. It is open nakedness and hidden mystery. It is joyful tears on a honeymooner's face. It is tears on a wrinkled face on a golden wedding anniversary.

"Sex is a quiet look across a room, a love note on a pillow, a rose lying on a breakfast plate, laughter in the night. Sex is life, not all of life, but wrapped up in the meaning of life. Sex is Your good gift, oh God, to enrich life, to continue the race, to communicate, to show me who I am, to reveal my mate, to cleanse through one flesh.

"Lord, some people say that sex and religion do not mix, but your word says that sex is good. Help me to keep it good in my life. Help me to be open about sex and still protect its mystery. Help me to see that sex is neither demon nor deity. Help me not to climb into a fantasy world with an imaginary sexual partner. Help me in the real world to love the people whom You have created.

"Teach me that my soul does not have to frown at sex for me to be a Christian. It is hard for many people to say, 'Thank God for sex' because for them, sex is more of a problem than a gift. They

need to know that sex and gospel can be linked together again. They need to hear the good news about sex. Show me how I can help them. Thank You, Lord, for making me a sexual being. Thank You for showing me how to treat others with trust and love. Thank You for letting me talk to You about sex. Thank You that I feel free to say, 'Thank God for sex.'"

Learn about Christian sexuality. Give yourself to truth. Cleave to understanding in your spirit until it becomes a life-giving principle. Separate the world's cheap imitations from that which is like gold in its value. Intimacy is the essence of expression. Rightly understood, God-given sexuality is both a refuge and a resource.

8

GOD MADE MAN

A bishop of the Methodist Church, Bishop Candler, was a short, stocky man. When someone asked him why he didn't play golf, he said, "Well, I have a problem. If I get close enough to hit the ball, I can't see it because of my stomach. If I get far enough away to see it, I can't reach the ball to hit it."

We often find ourselves in somewhat the same dilemma. We know where the problem is, but if we get close enough to do anything about it, we can't see it. But when we get far enough away to see the problem in its right perspective, we cannot touch it. The problems of this world seem almost insurmountable. We have created a society where it is virtually impossible for people to be what God intended.

When I was a seventeen-year-old boy, God called me to a spiritual understanding of men and women. While I may not feel some of their hurts by experience, I believe that I am like Jesus in the respect that the Bible says, "He was touched with the feelings of our infirmities." I have learned to feel what other people feel. I hope somehow to convey an understanding of men the way God created them.

Women can't live without men; therefore, they must learn to live with them. The best way to learn about men is to try to understand them. How do we know a man? How do we learn about a man? No college course offers the answers. Unless one gets into certain types of psychological or sociological research, the chances of knowing the psychological makeup of a particular man are very remote. Through spiritual discernment, I hope to reveal insights into man's makeup from the eyes of a man, the eyes of a woman and the eyes of God.

We look at man as a very complicated being, yet he is surprisingly simple. He is probably so simple that most people have overlooked some obvious things. One of the first statements we read in the Bible is, "God made man." I believe that when God made man, He made man singularly. He was an incomplete and insufficient creature with great needs. Because man was alone, God made someone else to complete him.

"God made man in His own likeness and in His image." That statement says much about a man if we stopped right there. God gave man dominion. He made him with an innate characteristic to rule, to cover, to protect and to supply. He told man to "name the other creatures." God gave man an intrinsic capacity for certain kinds of responsibilities. Unless a man finds a place to express himself properly, his gifts from God become corrupted. Corrupted dominion is often expressed in cruel behavior.

Some women have been the recipients of either mental or physical brutality because a man did not know how to take dominion peoperly. If a woman knew how to teach and help that man, he would not be cruel. There are exceptions, of course, but I am speaking concerning most situations of misdirected dominion. A frustrated man can become cruel because he has no one over whom he can rule and reign. Men must have dominion and be protectors and providers of covering. Our society has almost completely taken authority away from the man. At the turn of the century, most people lived on farms, and the male grew the crops and hunted to provide food for his family. He built his own house to protect his family. In that lifestyle, he had the opportunity to fulfill his need to be a provider and a protector.

A basic problem among men in our society is that they no longer feel needed. Women have become much too self-sufficient. A man is not satisfied because he wants a woman to need him. Many times the marriage bed is defiled because a wife becomes a sexual convenience without fulfilling a husband's emotional needs. He becomes frustrated.

Understand that man did not create himself. He was created in a specific way. When God's intentions are frustrated or prostituted, a man becomes very insensitive and that insensitivity can turn his life in wrong directions. He either totally forsakes his responsibili-

161

ties or becomes too aggressive. The basic principle is that God made man in His likeness and in His image and God said, to him, "Take care of creation. Be a steward to the earth."

To estrange a father from a growing child is a very grave error. He may grumble and complain because the child gets candy on his shirt or knocks the paper out of his hands, but deep inside he wants that child to need him. When a woman becomes the corrector, the disciplinarian and the provider for the children, she builds walls around them that seem to say, "I am the only parent you need." Many men are tremendously frustrated as parents. Therapy groups for abused wives and children exist today because men become cruel and express themselves in unnatural ways because of their frustrations.

A man is a little boy. Time has lengthened his arms and legs, but he is still a little boy and he always will be. If wives don't let their husbands be little boys with them, they will be little boys with someone else. He is going to have a playmate. If his wife is not his playmate, he will find another one and become even more frustrated. He may have very high morals, but the little boy characteristics remain and must be expressed in some way.

Men must live out their "youth" mentality. A man has youthful aggressiveness. He searches to find out who he is and what he is all about. He has to express desires that he did not necessarily create. A "youth" mentality is directed by desires. If those desires are not fulfilled and satisfied properly, a man becomes abusive and sometimes abnormal in his actions.

Is he to blame because he has desires? Why does a man get out of balance? Does a man have to accept a lack of satisfaction in his life? Perhaps the main frustration is caused simply because he is not needed by a woman. Without oneness in relationships, a man can never know true fulfillment. He becomes just a convenience to his family, and that attitude coming from a woman is devastating to a man.

A man is still a little boy who needs to run to his mother's breast. He is going to get hurt and cry on somebody's shoulder even if he must hire a prostitute. He will say to her, "My wife doesn't understand me." That happens every day because a wife didn't see the little boy in her husband who needed to be comforted by her.

I recently counseled a couple who had gotten to a total impasse in their marriage. The man was 6'1", weighed about 200 pounds, and seemed to be totally self-sufficient. He was a highly educated man who taught other people. His wife was a very warm, outgoing woman who had found another relationship because of his insensitivity. I asked God to give me discernment. They were not from my church, therefore I had to discern by the Spirit many of the problems in the relationship.

I began to see that this man was just a grown-up little boy. Inwardly, he was hurting and confused. He appeared confident, but privately he had no place to cry and receive understanding from someone. What he really wanted was to be taken into his wife's arms and to be allowed to cry. He needed to hear, "I love you," and to be comforted like a little child. Here sat a stern, strong, seemingly impenetrable man with a quivering chin and tears running down his cheeks.

That wife looked at her husband and said, "I didn't know you could cry." They had been married for fifteen years and she didn't know he could be broken. She had never created the circumstances for him to be vulnerable enough to cry. Men are little boys, youths who have great desires that may go in any direction. They can be improperly directed toward selfish satisfactions. Many men have no particular goals except just to be satisfied.

Any desire that is an end in itself is always evil. A desire must have an ultimate goal. If we eat only to satisfy our appetites, we lose the meaning of eating. Too many "live to eat." When we learn to "eat to live," we will correct our diets. The major concern should not be what size clothing a woman or man wears. Cancer and other horrible diseases are rampant in society because we do not eat to live—we live to eat.

If the basic reason for sexual intimacy is simply to satisfy that physical desire, sex becomes legalized masturbation. When a man feels that he does not really need a woman for any purpose beyond sexual desire, a woman becomes like a used piece of equipment to be laid aside until she is needed again. Sexual desire alone never produces true integration of two people into one spirit.

A man, with a "youth" mentality and desires, must learn that there is fulfillment beyond the satisfaction of that physical desire. Sex prior to marriage becomes a tremendous evil because it teaches young people to simply satisfy their desires. Pre-marital sex is not an experience leading toward a more meaningful relationship. Great damage to true fulfillment in this day is caused by the "new morality" that our society has sanctioned. God created natural sexual desires within us to be enjoyed within the covenant of marriage.

A woman is deceived if she believes that a man is her property because she has a piece of paper saying that he belongs to her. Wrong! People can have a marriage contract, but that partner doesn't necessarily belong to a husband or wife. A husband belongs to his wife only because she satisfies all of him, the little boy, the youth and finally, the mature man.

If a man cannot provide for his wife, he finds someone else for whom he can provide protection and covering. The need to provide may be manifested in unusual ways. He may take treats to the office every day because something inside him needs to provide for a person who appreciates his thoughtfulness. He wants to experience the appreciation from one for whom he has provided. Although a woman works, she must make a man feel needed by finding areas where she proves that she cannot get along without him.

We will be judged by God according how we handle relationships. We are not judged by God according to the number of times we lift our hands in praise, how much we read the Word or how many times we fasted or prayed. The total law and the prophets are built upon two principles by which we are judged: how we treat God and how we treat others. God's judgment is that simple. We can try to spiritualize or ignore truth, but those criteria are the essence of God's judgment.

The areas of a man's life, if not satisfied, erupt in corruption of society. The little boy in a man needs to be comforted. He needs to be mothered by a woman, but he

165

would never openly acknowledge that need. Every man has physiological and emotional needs that he does not know how to address. Because he does not know how to meet these needs, he becomes frustrated and confused and misuses his emotions. Satisfying his needs becomes a goal in itself. A man may live out his life without understanding why God placed certain desires within him.

A variety of characters in the Bible represent many different kinds of men, but all of them had the same needs. The great man of faith, Abraham, needed a Sarah. David, a frustrated king who was the apple of God's eye had certain kinds of needs that had never been expressed. While we must regard David's sin as evil, the fact is that David felt an emptiness inside. God would not have granted him grace or allowed him to have Bathsheba and their son, who later became the king, if this were not true. God always punishes transgressions, but an even deeper understanding of God is shown through His grace. The psalmist said, "He knoweth my frame." Because God knew David and saw his repentant spirit, He continued to use him.

The Apostle Paul seemed at times to be prejudiced against women. When we study Paul very carefully, we find that he had been hurt. While Paul was the great apostle, many needs were evident in his life which he obviously didn't know how to address. Yet to show his basic need for women, he wrote, "Bless the women who served me there and helped me." His epistles usually closed with a comment to certain women. Because he could not live in a one-to-one relationship, he accepted women on another basis. If we understand Paul's humanity even though he was an apostle, we will have a greater appreciation for his teaching on marriage.

The Word of God is filled with people just like us. We don't find one man in the entire Bible in whose life God did not expose some area of sin except Jesus who "became sin for us" (II Corinthians 5:21). Even Daniel said of himself, "I am a sinful man because I have not prayed as I should." Is it possible to imagine Daniel saying that? God always works with mankind in whatever condition He finds us.

The Bible is a story of how God works with people in their problems, inadequacies and victories. The lives of these men are like a thread which runs throughout the Bible. Men need to be leaders. They need to be accepted and comforted. They need to be understood. If Paul could have had a woman to comfort him properly, he possibly would not have had to defend himself at times by saying, "Have I become your enemy? Bear with me in my folly, but let me tell you this about myself." No, that need to express frustration might not have been so great if he had known proper comfort at home. But God used Paul's frustrations to teach us about problems in mankind.

Every man needs to be comforted and needed. He needs to feel wanted, understood and loved in spite of his inadequacies. The tremendous rise today in homosexuality, especially lesbianism, has happened because Satan wants to prostitute the male-female relationship to such a degree that the final blow is dealt when women say, "We really don't need you." There are situations when women need to comfort one another, but beyond a certain level, ministry between women becomes abnormal and damaging. Wise leadership in the Body of Christ understands the advantages of placing godly men in the role of covering and counseling rather than allowing certain feelings to be channeled only through women.

Any kind of love relationship involves risks, but love is worth the risk. Spiritual love relationships are the only way God can provide healing in the Body of Christ. We should transcend one-on-one relationships to come into a "Body relationship." The Church that Jesus is building can say to the world, "I will become a father to you because you need provision and covering. Through my incarnation in human beings, I will become a husband to you or a wife to you. Some of your needs have to be met spiritually. Dangers always exist, but God wants to bring healing."

How did Jesus know about women when He was never involved with women? He was involved with His mother, sisters and many other women, including Mary Magdalene who was a prostitute. The Pharisees refused to believe that Jesus was a prophet because He was the friend of a woman with a bad reputation. Jesus was as involved with those the world labeled "evil women" as He was with good women. Because He loved them, they became good women. In God's grace and His incarnation, Jesus accomplished the miraculous through relationships. When He hung on the cross, who was there? Women! In Jesus's dying hours, He remembered one special woman, His mother. The interaction between Jesus and women has not changed in the Church today. The Apostle Paul, whom we sometimes believe did not understand women, defines "pure religion" as taking care of widows and orphans.

A man wants to be a leader and a provider, but he should not be undermined by his wife. She should help him so that he can be the best provider possible.

He is like a little boy who is too old for the bottle but wants it when he goes to bed. He doesn't want anybody else to know his needs. Men don't want people to know that they are "little boys" so they cover their true emotions with a hard veneer. They become "know it all's." Many men make unreasonable demands of women because the "little boy" in him doesn't want anybody else to know he is a "little boy."

I recently attended a meeting with Christian world leaders. One session was was given to just "being vulnerable" to one another. Such an experience is frightening for leaders with great responsibility, especially when we speak to thousands of people and are supposed to be authorities in Christian circles. One leader said, "People look upon me as an educated man with many answers. I am called 'Doctor,' but I was a high school drop-out. I am very insecure. When I am in a meeting, I immediately feel that I must 'take over.' Down inside, I am still a high school drop-out who wants to be accepted. The greatest need in my life was met when you men accepted me without asking questions." Men don't want anyone to know their insecurities. A grandfather, father, or brother will not tell anyone that he has needs.

If a husband does not have a daughter, he must learn some things from someone else's daughter. A wife must allow him that freedom without becoming jealous. If a man has not raised a son, his wife must encourage him to be close to someone else's son. Understanding is God-given.

What attitudes war against fulfillment? Evil emotions. Jealousy. Possessiveness. These responses are soulish and destructive. Women can tell their husbands that they are unhappy with them without expressing those feelings verbally. All a wife has to do is "shrug" a certain way, and her body language immediately tells her husband how she really feels. When she shows him that he was wrong by closing him out of her life, she takes away his manhood.

It is never too late in a marriage for a woman to recognize her husband's role and open her heart to him. The door may appear to be closed, but a woman must learn from her failures. Hurts in marital relationships often end in separation and divorce. Sometimes divorce is the only solution, but not nearly as often as statistics indicate. Divorce must be considered only after problems have been thoroughly examined, and even then as a last resort. When a problem has not been solved, that problem will always arise in other relationships. We must define the problems and determine how to cope with them. Sometimes through an honest examination of problems, a marriage can be saved, but insoluble problems must be dealt with so that others will not be hurt later.

Don't be ashamed to address problems wherever they are encountered. It is never too late to discover the innate characteristics that God has placed within man. Learn to cope with selfish desires and to consider the needs of others. If a woman is going to live and work in a society with men, she needs to learn something about them. She needs discernment to know whether a man is abusive or simply hurt. What feelings exist within a man? What are his needs? Although we are not married to the people we work with, we still must relate to them. We need to understand the boss who "barks out" commands because he is frustrated at home. He desperately needs to convince himself that he is needed. Christians must become the peacemakers in our society.

A man absolutely must be "the king" in somebody's life, and every "king" must have a "queen." That "king" needs to be recognized, accepted, wanted and desired. He must never be called a "brute" or a "beast" because he has desires which God created him to have.

Remember, God made man. God made man with all of his desires, needs and ambitions. If women intend to cooperate with God in the Kingdom, they must learn God's intentions. We must learn the reasons that God made man as He did. These answers are at the heart of the Kingdom of God. As Christians we can never correct an abused world until we know why God made man. We need to see ourselves honestly. We must understand our callings and God's purposes.

Don't get circumstances and purposes confused. Most of the time, people get bogged down in their circumstances. Most people judge their lives on the basis of their circumstances, not in terms of their purposes. Paul said, "I have finished my course. My life had a purpose" (II Timothy 4:7). Jesus said, "Toward this end, I was born" (John 18:37).

Do we know why we were born? Why did God make a particular person a woman, or make another individual a man? Don't violate God's creative processes by saying, "God, You didn't know what You were doing. I should have been a man." A woman who says that has an identity problem and is in trouble. Our frustrations usually arise because we have not learned why God made us. Sometimes we put too much emphasis on one area and cause the rest of our lives to be out of balance. Success in one area makes us forget that the rest of our lives are not fulfilled. When we have done the best we can do, God will be the first one to say, "Great! Grand! Glorious!"

9

GOD MADE WOMAN

God created a helpmeet for Adam, a partner who would fit into his plans. That meaning of "helpmeet" is probably closest to the original writings (Genesis 2:18). Women are not less important because they fit into someone else's plans. The Word of God records how valuable women are in the work of God. In Genesis 1:26, the word "them" means more than one. Man and woman are both necessary to complete God's purposes in headship. It seems, therefore, that God's original plan was to make man, male and female.

And the Lord God said, "It is not good that man should be alone; I will make him a helper comparable to him." (Genesis 2:18)

Then God said, "Let us make man in Our image, according to Our likeness; let them have dominion over the fish of the sea, over the birds of the air, and over the cattle, over all the earth and over every creeping thing that creeps on the earth." So God created man in His own image; in the image of God He created him; male and female He created them. (Genesis 1:26-27)

A simple analogy to demonstrate oneness in man, male and female, is to consider that an apple cut in half produces two edible pieces. Both pieces have a separate form, but to become a whole apple, they must be put back together. I believe that in the eyes of God, man is both male and female. They are inseparable. Our problem has been that we have never quite understood this concept of oneness. Man has gone his way and woman has gone her way. Great frustration occurs for both sexes because we have not learned to fit our lives together.

When people in a Kingdom Church learn how to fit together as a whole unit, God can accomplish His purposes in the earth. That process is painful. The whole earth groans for the complete truth to fulfill our roles in God's plan.

We are God's messengers to the world. Before we can proclaim His message, we must understand two things. God made man, male and female, and He has distinct purposes for both. Why did God create man, male and female? God was lonely. Until we learn to be totally vulnerable to another person, we will never be content. Unfortunately, that person is not always a husband or wife.

Loneliness can occur when one is in the midst of hundreds of people. Loneliness is the result of never having been totally known by someone. If we really understood this concept, we would greatly reduce the need for psychiatric or psychological counseling because proper relationships answer basic human needs. Why did God make us male and female? A need for help is so basic in human beings that we all must have interaction in order to fulfill our purposes. God made woman to complete man. The two of them became "man" in the sight of God. Fellowship and interaction are absolute necessities for human fulfillment. Mutual sharing should always be the central part of a marriage. A wife who functions independently frustrates her husband because God made her to be his helper. Until a woman fulfills her role as a "helpmeet," she will always be frustrated and never know why she was made.

Our society is structured in direct opposition to God's plan. Educational institutions encourage a unisex concept. Every goal taught by humanistic theories of social order encourages independence. The Bible says, "Be not conformed to this world." A transformed woman understands her role in God's plan. Understanding comes only through a transformed mind. Carnal women—women who are not born of the Spirit—cannot understand God's purposes. A transformed woman understands that she must always fulfill the role of a helpmeet. When she does not function as a helper, she will become frustrated. If we try to become something other than what God intended us to be, fulfillment is impossible.

Woman was not an afterthought to God. Woman was in God's heart and mind from the very beginning of creation. He made man, male and female. "And the Lord God said, 'It is not good that man should be alone;

I will make him a helper comparable to him' " (Genesis 2:18). God initiated interaction and vulnerability with us, just as the Holy Spirit wants intimate interaction with His creation even today.

Out of the ground the Lord God formed every beast of the field and every bird of the air, and brought them to Adam to see what he would call them. And whatever Adam called each living creature, that was its name. So Adam gave names to all cattle, to the birds of the air, and to every beast of the field. But for Adam there was not found a helper comparable to him. (Genesis 2:19-20)

The animals were made from the ground as Adam had been, but they could not help him. They could amuse him, entertain him and fascinate him, but they could not help him as his equal.

And the Lord God caused a deep sleep to fall on Adam, and he slept; and He took one of his ribs, and closed up the flesh in its place. Then the rib which the Lord God had taken from man He made into a woman, and He brought her to the man. (Genesis 2:21-22)

Out of the ground, God made the beasts of the field. Out of Adam, to become bone of his bone and flesh of his flesh, God made woman.

And Adam said: "This is now bone of my bones and flesh of my flesh; she shall be called Woman, because she was taken out of Man." Therefore a man shall leave his father and mother and be joined to his wife, and they shall become one flesh. (Genesis 2:23-24)

A mystery in God's Word is the spiritual fulfillment of this creation of man and woman in the New Testament Church. "And they were both naked, the man and his wife, and were not ashamed" (Genesis 2:25). What a refreshing thought! She could not have existed apart from him. Many people think that marriage only means signing a contract. A marriage license exists for society's sake, for legal aspects of ownership and for the protection of and provision for children. Marriage is God's will, but unfortunately, balance and fulfillment do not always exist in marriage. A contract has nothing to do with God's purposes in marriage. God wants commitment, but contracts cannot insure solid relationships.

The Bible says, "And they were naked." That description gives insight into the right relationship that man and woman had with one another. They were not ashamed before God. If we stand before God ashamed and without confidence, the reason is that we are not in right relationships. Nobody may know the problem but that person and God. We put on spiritual clothes and do away with guilt by comprehending spiritual truths.

A spiritual mystery that many people have never understood is written in Ephesians: "Wives, submit to your own husbands as to the Lord" (Ephesians 5:22). That spiritual concept does not apply if the husband is not like the Lord. A woman who does not have a spiritually-minded husband should submit to him only in natural areas. Unfortunately, she cannot submit to him in spiritual things. She can maintain a home and do those things that are proper and right in the sight of God with the hope and purpose of eventually bringing her husband to God. Without that purpose in a

177

partner's life, the marriage would be meaningless. Although that marriage may suffer torment and tragedy, the purpose in her heart causes her to become an intercessor for her husband. Her purpose for staying in the marriage is to redeem him according to I Corinthians 7. She becomes like the Israelite handmaiden to bring him to the Lord.

For the husband is head of the wife, as also Christ is head of the church; and He is the Savior of the body. Therefore, just as the church is subject to Christ, so let the wives be to their own husbands in everything. (Ephesians 5:23-24)

This verse is talking about a spiritual head to whom God has given a helper. "Husbands, love your wives, even as Christ also loved the church and gave Himself for it." A woman cannot submit herself spiritually to a man who does not give himself for her. If he is selfish and self-centered, if he goes his own way by disregarding God's ways, she cannot submit to that man. He has not given himself to his wife, his family or God. His wife cannot submit to him because she always feels fear and mistrust in the relationship. The part of her which needs spiritual fellowship is always vacant and inactive because she as a spiritual woman cannot submit to him.

"That He might sanctify and cleanse it with the washing of water by the word" (Ephesians 5:26). To some degree we can cleanse and sanctify relationships. We can cleanse and sanctify those companions and relationships that God gives to us. The purpose is "that He might present it to Himself a glorious Church." This scripture is talking about the Church, using the example of marriage to give us understanding.

Paul said that which is natural is first. That which is natural sets the patterns for the spiritual from which we learn about God's purposes. "Doth not nature itself teach you?" Paul is teaching not only a lesson about marriage, but also about the Church as well.

That He might present it to Himself a glorious church, not having spot or wrinkle or any such thing, but that it should be holy and without blemish. So husbands ought to love their own wives as their own bodies; he who loves his wife loves himself. For no one ever hated his own flesh, but nourishes and cherishes it, just as the Lord does the church. (Ephesians 5:27-29)

What did God say about Adam and Eve? She was bone of his bone and flesh of his flesh. Now we are members of Christ's Body. A husband-wife relationship should mirror Christ and the Church. As the Church, we are bone of His bone and flesh of His flesh. Paul is talking about the Church and not the relationship between a man and woman. Christ places us within a Body relationship as His Church.

"Therefore a man shall leave his father and mother and be joined to his wife, and the two shall become one flesh" (Genesis 2:24; Ephesians 5:51). Again, this verse refers to the spiritual relationship between a man and woman, but an even greater truth is found in the next verse. "This is a great mystery, but I speak concerning Christ and the church."

Everything in this passage illustrates how Christ and His Church are interrelated as members of one Body. We are so joined together that nothing can separate us. Neither life nor death nor powers nor principalities nor relationships nor anything is able to separate those who are one in His Spirit. Many people do not understand that. They are led to devastation by not knowing how to separate submission in their natural lives without losing their spiritual relationships in the Body of Christ.

Perhaps a Christian wife is married to a man who is a good husband and father, but he does not share his wife's commitment to the Lord. She must recognize the differences between the dimensions of oneness in spiritual and natural relationships. This situation is very common in the Church and calls for great maturity in a woman's love and spiritual commitment both to her husband and to the Church. A woman who is spiritually mature can use her God-given warmth and sexuality to reveal God's love to her husband. I know this may seem like a bold statement to many people, but I am convinced that this plan is advocated by Paul in I Corinthians 7.

The mystery is that we have become "bone of bone" to one another. We have become "flesh of flesh" to one another and are inseparable except through willful disobedience and rebellion. In the next verse, Paul adds almost as an afterthought, "I have been talking about the Church."

Nevertheless let each one of you in particular so love his own wife as himself, and let the wife see that she respects her husband. (Ephesians 5:33)

Jesus did not come to bring peace. He said, "I come to bring a sword." Jesus promised great strife in family relationships — brother turning against brother, father against son, mother against daughter — because each person obeys a different set of rules.

We are members of His body, flesh of His flesh and bone of His bone. This explains the prayer Jesus prayed in John 17:21, "I pray, Father, that you make them one—bone of bone and flesh of flesh—interrelated in such a way that they are inseparable in persecution, nakedness and famine." That unity must precede the establishment of the Kingdom of God.

Jesus prayed, "Father, make them one." When we comprehend oneness, we must learn by the Spirit where to draw the line between spiritual relationships, spiritual involvement and spiritual authority as opposed to fleshly and natural relationships. We must recognize spiritual boundary lines or Satan will overthrow us. Either Satan attempts to cause us to compromise our spiritual natures, or we become so spiritual that we do not fulfill our natural responsibilities. Either of these extremes is wrong.

I have seen women through the eyes of women all of my life. Women see other women in ways that "compare themselves among themselves," and their comparisons are never an accurate appraisal. Women never get so spiritual that they are able to see another woman objectively because they, too, are women. "Only your hairdresser knows for sure" is an accurate statement. Anybody else who tells a woman how her hair looks, good or bad, usually is not telling the truth. Women don't dress for men, they dress for other women.

Women usually dress, put on make-up and have their stiff coiffeurs to impress other women. They never do all that for men, never! Not part of the time . . . never! A woman would usually not ask a man, "How does this dress look?" except to be nice to him. She wants her women friends to say, "Ah, that dress looks great!" "Those shoes look great," and she looks down at her friend's shoes to see if they look like hers.

Women get a new style of glasses, and other women look at their own glasses and want them to look like their friend's. She never asks her husband, "Do those glasses look good on me?" She doesn't really care what he thinks because she's dressing for other women. Other women's opinions always cheat her because usually they want to look better than she does. If they can keep a woman from looking good, they will possibly look better than she.

The way a woman speaks can make another person feel either good or bad. Our feelings are dependent upon how other people respond to us. That response causes peer pressure. We fuss about our teenagers having peer pressure at school and their insistence on wearing Jordache jeans, Izod sweaters and Polo shirts. We accuse them of following the traditions of the world, yet a woman competes with every other woman she meets. Peer pressure? We are not governed by God's intentions in making woman as a helper to her husband. God never told women to help other women with the way they looked. Never once. The Church is supposed to please God; women are supposed to please their husbands.

Many women are negative and emotional. They go by their feelings because they are judged by the wrong criteria. Negative emotions, jealousy and competition rule their lives. Women who play tennis together are highly competitive. If a woman plays tennis with a man, she's not nearly as competitive. Down in her heart, she knows that even if they both play their best, in that area he'll probably win. She may act like she's competing, but down inside she isn't. It takes away the strain.

Men are built to compete because God created them to be in authority. Frustration arises when women don't understand that submission is a natural, innate quality within them. Competitiveness in women reveals that they have acquired some masculine qualities. Women have a natural desire to want to come in second in competition with men. If a woman makes a higher score than her date in some game or activity, she has little satisfaction in winning. Besides, she will frustrate him.

Few scripture references concern woman-to-woman relationships. One Biblical concept is that spiritual mothers should have spiritual daughters, but never do the scriptures condone spiritual competitiveness between them. Naomi did not compete with Ruth. The story of Ruth is an excellent demonstration of a proper relationship between two women. Women's relationships should be based in terms of advice and encouragement. Naomi, the older woman in this story, is an example of the Holy Spirit in Ruth's life.

Older and younger women should relate to each other. The Bible says that older women should teach younger women how to love their husbands, thereby teaching them how to love Christ. Through their marriage relationships, women learn how to love and submit to the Church. If they are able to submit to a sincere, spiritual man, they will very easily submit to God and to the Church.

Competitiveness in our daughters keeps them from a proper understanding of their responsibilities toward their husbands and the Church. They will eventually be devastated and destroyed by attitudes of competitiveness.

How does a man see a woman? I will divide this discussion into two categories. First, I will explore how a carnal man sees women; and secondly, how a spiritual man sees women. A carnal man sees a woman as a sex object. There is no other way to describe his perceptions. She is a convenience. She exists to gratify him, not necessarily to help him.

Carnal attraction is a basic magnetism between a man and a woman. On that basis, a relationship will cool when a wife becomes physically unattractive or has a physical problem which prohibits sexual activity. This relationship is not built on love. Nothing really sustains the relationship beyond physical attraction. Christian women should never marry a carnal man. Never! They should live out their lives as single women submitted to the Church rather than marry a carnal man.

Secondly, a carnal man regards a woman as a servant. If she doesn't keep his house and clothes properly, or do anything that he wants her to do, he becomes angry. He has no ability to understand her as anything but a personal servant. A man's spirituality can be judged by the view that he has of his wife. A carnal man sees a woman as a sex object, a servant and also as a weaker vessel.

Peter strongly warned men to be careful about how they treat what he calls "the weaker vessel" because

184

thoughtless behavior will hinder their prayers. Relationships always either impede or strengthen our spiritual communion with God.

Finally, the carnal man sees women as a necessary evil. He wants the companionship of a woman to gratify his flesh. There are no exceptions. The natural man cannot love with spiritual affections. He may play games occasionally, but he cannot live in a spiritual relationship. Whether he wants to love spiritually or not, he cannot. That which is flesh is flesh, and that which is spirit is spirit. One is always controlled by the other.

The natural man will abuse women mentally or physically, sometimes even to the point of rape or forcing their wills to gain personal gratification. He treats women as "second class citizens." Prejudice against women stems from the basic attitudes of natural, carnal men.

Sincere, spiritual men view women as Christ views the Church. A truly spiritual man regards a woman as his helper. This concept transcends friendship or any other kind of relationship because the identities of man and woman become inseparable. The woman fits into his plans. He cannot fulfill his plans without her. She becomes his mother if he needs mothering. If he needs a lover, she's his lover. If he needs a wife and companion, the woman is a gift that God has given to him as a friend.

A wife must also become the flesh woman that her husband needs. If she doesn't, he will get out of balance in his life. That does not mean he will compromise his principles. He won't necessarily become a drug addict, an alcoholic or read pornographic material to satisfy his needs. But she must learn how to make him touch the earth. A woman is a heavenly creation to him, but she is also an earthly creation with both spiritual and natural resources. The wife should be the one who teaches her husband how to touch the earth through her mind, rather than through his own.

A woman's role is different from a man's, but she is equal in dominion and rule. Christ said that the Church is His co-ruler. Likewise, a woman becomes co-ruler with her husband.

The greatest friend that God ever made for the natural woman was the Church. God gave her dominion through her abilities to discern and have spiritual influence. When Esther's spirit touched the king, the king said, "Half the kingdom is yours." That promise is prophetic. Women can change the world if they understand this concept.

Pastors should be the ones teaching principles of family relationships in family seminars. Biblical concepts concerning relationships belong to the Church. Carnal minds cannot even comprehend God's ways. The Church has been remiss in addressing these issues because it lacked the courage to speak the truth.

A woman has dominion with the man. Usually she is most effective in the areas of discernment and influence. Any man who becomes vulnerable will admit that he wants a woman to rule with him. He wants to say, "Half of my kingdom is yours." Every king must have a queen. If he sees himself as a son of God, what does that identity give his wife? She becomes the daughter of the King. If he is a spiritual man, he will view her as the other half of himself. The spirituality of a man is evident by his image of a spiritual women. If he never accepts her role of authority, he doesn't properly understand her role. He is afraid of her discernment and influence.

A spiritual man is never impressed with a woman's material assets. He is only impressed by her becoming the spiritual woman that God intended her to be. She will always desire to fit into his plans. Wives who don't fit into their husbands' plans become disappointed and frustrated with themselves.

How does God see a woman? God sees women exactly as he created them: a man who is divided into two parts. That's the only way God can see either men or women. Any other concept is less than God's plan. God sees the whole "man." Women are to relate as helpers both in the natural world and in the spiritual world.

Secondly, God sees women as those He created to have dominion. God sees her as one who will subdue the world. A woman will rule, reign and have dominion as a helper through her ability to discern and to intercede. Two great calls upon every Christian wife are to learn how to discern and to intercede for her husband.

When the body of Jesus lay in the tomb, women took spices to anoint Him and to minister to His body. A woman's call is to minister to the Body of Christ. Transcend the two-part relationship of a man and a wife and look at a woman as God sees her: the other part of spiritual headship. Women are half of spiritual authority in the Church because of their abilities to discern and intercede. Discernment and intercession transcend natural abilities. Some women are praisers.

I can praise God to a certain dimension, but I can also enter into the praise of an anointed woman who freely magnifies the Lord. I enter into music and praise through those who lead in worship. I've learned to trust women's discernment and intercession.

Until we reclaim the kingdoms of this earth, Jesus Christ cannot return. Women must support their husbands with intercession as they battle together for the cause of the Kingdom. Women are to stand strong with discernment, understanding and praise.

Men should make decisions. They sit in the council rooms. That's not usually a woman's calling. God told her to pray for men of authority who can make the right decision. When a woman tries to dominate a decision-making process, she usually becomes frustrated.

The third way that God sees a woman is as His maturing bride. He looks upon her as the first example. Understand that women symbolize the Bride of Christ. Of course, men are part of the Bride of Christ also, but women have the spirits of Miriam and Esther. A man cannot, as a natural man, be an example of a bride. As a bride, men must fit into the women's example just as she fits into his example in other areas. Women must begin to symbolize the Bride with beauty, grace and patience.

Man is created to make decisions and take command. God has called a woman to implement a man's ideas. He sees her as a bride, but remember, the bride is called to please her husband. If she tries to take his place, she will destroy the role that God has created him to assume. An unsubmitted woman has the power to destroy her husband.

Don't try to take a husband's place. I believe a dangerous situation exists when a woman makes more money than her husband. He may never tell her, but if he's able to support the family, allow him do it. Wisdom for a woman is to always be one step behind her husband. If a woman is working on a big project, let a man think he's the one who planned it.

A woman must be what God intended her to be. She may be surprised at what men really want. A man loves simplicity. Usually, he doesn't like gourmet foods on a regular basis. Most men really like basic foods such as beans, potatoes, ham, fried chicken, cornbread and blackeyed peas. Fancy foods frustrate him because man is really a very simple creation.

A godly woman should have the Deborah spirit so that she knows how to judge, discern, speak with authority and move without fear, but first she must understand the message of the Church today.

I beg women to be not only like Deborah, but also to be like the Israelite maiden who knew God's voice and plans. The little girl told the wife of the Syrian captain, "Naaman, I know God's plan. God's plan is revealed in the words of that prophet over there." Do women believe that God still has a prophet and a prophetic voice? Are they intimidated by saying that God has a prophetic voice? Are they willing to say, "God does have prophetic voices today"? Women must be able to say boldly, "There is a prophet who can speak God's plan to us."

Joseph had God's plan. He knew how to save the nation. Daniel had God's plan. Somebody had to be the one to say, "Why, there's a boy in prison over there named Joseph. He knows the answer." Jesus said, "When the Spirit of truth comes, He will guide you into all truth."

A spirit of truth must guide us. Don't be be ashamed to be like an Israelite maiden or to be a Naomi. Naomi knew how to lead young women. Naomi knew how to give Ruth direction because she represented the Holy Spirit. Spiritual women represent the Holy Spirit to others because they have natural discernment and natural abilities that the Holy Spirit can use. Naomi told Ruth get into bed with Boaz. Imagine how that advice would be received today! "Get under his covering. Let him cover you." Spiritual women need to teach younger women how to stay under the covering of the Church.

Learn how to be an Esther. Understand that all of these qualities cannot be in one woman, but together they minister to the Body of Christ as a composite group. Some women will write about God's Kingdom. Others will write music. Some will sing, dance, praise and intercede because that's what God has made women to do. Become an Esther who rules half the Kingdom. Today a woman bears half the responsibility and half the curses, but one day she will rule half of the Kingdom.

The Bible said that Mary was able to keep secrets. She pondered in her heart the things of God that she didn't understand. She listened to the Lord. When God gave Mary instructions, she simply said, "Be it unto me as a handmaiden of the Lord." Learn to trust God in spite of circumstances and wait on the Lord. By her faith and trust, a woman brings a balance and a sense of security to the entire Body of Christ.

10

YOU DON'T BRING ME FLOWERS ANYMORE

Love songs often say things that we are thinking, but will not allow ourselves to say to someone we love. Remember the old song, "You Don't Bring Me Flowers Anymore"? I heard it again on the radio recently as I was riding along the highway. The song says, "You don't sing me love songs anymore." It also says something like, "You hardly talk to me anymore, although you used to talk to me about forever." The song concludes by saying, . . . "what used to be doesn't count anymore."

The words in this song disclose insights which help us to understand sentiments that keep intimate relationships alive. But even more importantly, I believe we can draw higher spiritual concepts from the song's message which God would like to put into our hearts to help us understand how we can express our love to Him in a more fulfilling way.

"You don't bring Me flowers anymore," God says to His Church. "You don't sing to Me anymore. You sing only to yourselves, and some of you don't sing at all. You don't talk to Me anymore. You don't pray. You don't have interaction with Me anymore. You're too busy doing your 'own thing.' You don't take time to have a date with Me anymore."

If God spoke those words directly to many Christians, they would quickly reply, "But, Lord, we prophesied in Your name. In Your name we did great things." But God's Word says that He would answer these rationalizations by saying, "I was naked and you didn't clothe Me. I was in prison and you didn't visit Me. I was made captive by society and you didn't understand My needs. I was hungry and you didn't feed Me. I sent prophets and you waited until they died to honor them by polishing their tombs. You don't bring Me flowers anymore."

History is "His story" about relationships. The entire Bible is about relationships which have the potential of glorifying God. An examination of relationships begins in the first chapter of Genesis. God wanted to relate to man. He created man, male and female, for companionship with each other and with Him. In their right relationship with God, He blessed them.

We all know the tragic story of broken relationships in the Garden of Eden. Eve didn't follow God's instructions. She even stood against Adam in her sin and deception and then Adam willfully followed her into sin against God. Through Adam's sin, relationships between man and God were entirely broken. We see rebellion lived out in their seed when Cain killed Abel.

The Word of the Lord is about carnal and spiritual relationships: Abraham's intercession over his nephew, Lot; David's desire for Uriah's wife, Bathsheba; Jesus as He pours Himself into His twelve disciples who often could not comprehend His vision; Martha, Mary and Lazarus in their close friendship with Jesus which resulted in resurrected life. The Bible even culminates relationships at a "marriage supper" of Christ and the Church in the Book of Revelation. We must understand that God created human beings to establish relationships. Our intimate love for Him makes going to church on Sunday far more than a ritual we simply think we are supposed to do. A "date" with God is more than just carrying out our traditions and being "religious."

The three dimensions of love we have already examined in human love — eros, philia and agape — can be lifted to dimensions of worship and praise to God. We love God at various dimensions. Examining these dimensions will help us to understand how we can love God with greater maturity to increase spiritual fruit in our lives. Love for God begins with a salvation experience. Until we understand that our love for God must grow beyond our gratitude for salvation, we will merely maintain an immature relationship with God which is far beneath His purposes for us.

First of all, let us examine "eros spirituality." I believe "eros worship," a bodily or physical worship, is instinctive within people. We physically express to God emotions, which are instinctive within us. We call that expression "praise." For a dancer, praise may be expressed in dancing. A singer will praise God in his songs. One who has rhythm in his body will begin to clap his hands. A person who is very pensive and perhaps somewhat inhibited may simply stand. All of these worshipers do whatever expression is instinctively right for them. Their expressions "feel" right. Eros worship feels right in our bodies. At whatever level we are free to praise God, we will feel comfortable in that expression. Sometimes the love for God in worship services never gets beyond an eros level. Is that evil or wrong? No, eros love is a beginning point from which to establish a mature love relationship with God.

Unless we understand levels of worship, we may believe that God desires only a physical response from us. We will remain immature lovers, responding to God only as One who meets our needs. I explained previously that a man who loves in a eros mentality will look at some woman and say, "I need you." Likewise, many people never grow beyond their own needs in worship. "I Need Thee Every Hour" is an old song that expresses this level of relationship with God. Individual needs are the absolute, total focus of eros worship.

Most people who worship at an eros level are what I call "up and down" Christians. If they don't feel "good" in their bodies and emotions, they may even question their own salvations. At an eros level of love for Jesus, Peter could say one moment, "Though all men forsake You, I will never leave You!" A few hours later, Peter would stand by the fire, cursing and denying that he even knew Jesus. Why? He lived in an eros love relationship with Jesus that was ruled by his emotions. Peter felt danger under negative pressure from others.

Eros love for God is based on whatever we feel. I have shared many times with my congregation about a time in my early ministry when I lived under a cloud of depression. For about five months, the Word of God was absolutely void of meaning to me. I preached every Sunday, at times not even believing in my mind that the Word of God was true. I knew God's love in my spirit, but my mind and emotions felt nothing. Sometimes when I got down to pray, I felt foolish. Yet I was the senior pastor of a large church. Engulfed in emotional depression, I didn't want to eat. I didn't have any desire to make love to my wife. Life lost all meaning. I was doing nothing that I knew was wrong, and yet I was totally wrong in my orientation because I didn't understand what was happening to me.

I was an absolute Pharisee. I would not admit the real world existed. I wouldn't even hit tennis balls in the late afternoon because I was afraid my congregation would criticize me for doing something I shouldn't do. If I watched television, I pulled one out of a closet because I didn't want my people to know I had a television set in my house. A person can never enter the Kingdom of God living in that sort of bondage.

Some people fall apart because they can't cope with the real world. In the midst of that experience, I stood on the Word of God because somewhere deep in my spirit, despite the external circumstances, I knew the Bible was true. I prayed because somehow I still knew prayer was the answer. But I honestly didn't feel anything. If I had continued requiring myself to experience an eros spirituality, I would have totally given up. That is the reason many people do give up and walk away from God.

Eros love is the level of many Christians' experiences with God. Eros love is related to one's feelings. It is related to whatever a person needs. When their needs are not met, Christians on the eros level get angry. Some folks come to a church unable to meet their house payments and say to a pastor, "Pay my house note for me." He replies, "I can't do it." They quickly answer, "Tra, la, la, I'm leaving!" They don't understand that what they really need is spiritual maturity. Many people come to church out of a basic sense of need. They seldom even consider asking God, "What am I going to give to You?"

The second level of spiritual love is expressed the Greek word "philia." Philia lovers simply make an arrangement with God for security reasons. The depth of their experience with God often determines their participation in the church. Once the extent of their participation has been established, they feel secure.

Philia worshipers usually have many friends who understand worship as they do. They have many people with whom they can talk about God. They are satisfied with their arrangement and their concept of Who God is. Their interaction with God is through intellectual agreement. They regard God as "doing His thing" while they "do their thing." This explanation may seem like an oversimplification, but this level characterizes most religious educational institutions. Philia love for God often blends well with the study of philosophy.

The marriage between philosophy and theology exists in so many places of higher education that we find difficulty in knowing where one ends and the other begins. Philosophy is the foundation of philia spirituality. Many people commit their lives to God through a deliberate intellectual decision. They simply make a deliberate commitment to the Lord. Evangelistic campaigns are often conducted on the basis of this spiritual goal.

"Come! Make a decision for Jesus Christ!" The choir sings twenty-five times, "Just as I am, without one plea." In many cases we might add the words, "And I'm going to stay this way the rest of my life." These believers have made a deliberate decision. Their decision is to get up, walk down an aisle, and say to a pastor, "I accept Jesus." I love those Christians, but that message without the full gospel is deceiving many people. Some Christians continue to grow and seek the Lord, but others stop right there at the altar. They never go beyond that "decision" encounter with Jesus.

Philia worshipers don't necessarily become tithers to the ministry. They seldom become givers of themselves in service to others. They just reach a level of understanding at which they make an intellectual decision. They understand that it's far better to say "yes" to Jesus Christ than to spend eternity in hell.

The third level of worship is what I call the "agape" spiritual life. I believe agape worship is God's plan and purpose for man. Agape worshipers don't attend church to see what they are going to get, but to discover what they can give to God. They walk into the church saying, "I want to give love to somebody tonight. I want to pray for somebody for healing. I want to en-

197

courage people tonight and make them feel loved and accepted. I'm not here to see whether anybody speaks to me. I want to speak to someone who is lonely or confused and needs a friend."

People will stand in line at the doors of a church filled with worshipers like that. Those worshipers will come eagerly to draw closer to the Lord by loving other people, not to find the most comfortable seats. They will walk down the aisle of the church with a sensitivity to the Holy Spirit saying, "Now, God, someone is here tonight who is hurting. Help me to find that person. Someone is here tonight who has been bruised in their relationships and they are brokenhearted. Jesus, I know that You came to heal the brokenhearted. Help me to find that person."

The Holy Spirit is God living in our fleshly bodies. Imagine the impact that a large group of people who have reached this level of spirituality could make in the world. Compassion is that essential foundation of agape love from God which flows through us to others. Jesus was moved with compassion. He asked the Father for nothing that would simply please Himself. He was moved with compassion when He saw the multitudes scattered. Compassion is the identifying mark of agape love.

As a matter of fact, agape love sees as God sees. It does not view God from an intellectual point of view, nor from a self-centered "feeling" perspective. Agape love sees as God sees. God always shepherds His people and He cares about their needs. God always understands exactly what needs to be ministered to people who seek Him. Agape worship is totally different from the worship we usually experience in churches today.

Agape worship may be loud and jubilant, or it may be quiet and reverent. We cannot project God's mood for any particular service. We only move as He leads us. We cannot simply plan to feel excitement or quiet reverence. We are totally directed in worship by the leading of the Holy Spirit.

I believe the kind of worship I'm describing is the worship which God seeks in His people. God seeks for people who worship Him in His Spirit so that we are in unity with Him. He desires to find true worshipers.

It is important that young people understand the differences in eros feelings of infatuation, philia love of intellectual, personal decisions and God-created, agape love. Agape love asks God for partners who can assist them in ministry. God has created a counterpart somewhere to complete each of us to accomplish His purposes in our lives.

I believe that a person's counterpart is not necessarily just one person, but God has a counterpart for everyone. I don't agree with some people who teach young people to go to God and say specifically, "God, I want a woman: five foot, six inches tall, 122¾ pounds, brown eyes or blue eyes, (that's not a big deal). But oh, God, I want her to be built!"

That request restricts God, doesn't it? Some young women pray, "Oh, Lord, I need a husband. Now, Lord, I don't want a short husband." What's wrong with a short husband? After all, there are some advantages to being short! Don't fight it without trying it. Too many people give God a description when they should be praying, "God, I need a counterpart in the Spirit who is the other half of who I am."

Imagine what would happen in marriages of the future if we taught our young people to approach their relationships by the Spirit. Imagine what would happen in young people's lives if they started saying, "God, you have an arrangement, a time, a place and a way. Help me to find Your will." Spiritual leaders must help young people to be sensitive in following the Spirit. Some Christians go to extremes. They become so spiritual that they wouldn't know their counterparts if God threw somebody at them! They have their eyes looking toward the sky, thinking they're going to be spiritual eunuchs. All they really become is pharisaical hypocrites.

The Kingdom of God is populated with people who have full consciousness. Kingdom people have a wholesome, realistic attitude about life. They face life wherever the issues are. They even recognize their own physical needs. It is not "spiritual" to say, "I don't have any sexual needs in my life." Kingdom people can say, "I know what my needs are. I know how I'm going to handle my needs in ways that will honor God. God will help me to do that." Then we must ask God to help us express our own desires in ways that brings life and edification to others.

In giving life, we gain life. This teaching is the very heart of God's love. I started praying sometime ago that the Lord would give me His heart for His people. I want to know God's heart. I believe the heart of God is when He says, "How can you love me when you don't love one another?" I believe God is saying to His people, "Learn what relationships are all about. Then you'll be able to relate to Me." We will never feel anything toward God that we cannot somehow feel in our relationships in the natural realm.

Across the years I have learned many things from my relationships with the people God has entrusted to me. I have observed that the more I interact with people and allow myself to feel life with them, the more tender I am when I preach. I believe that the reason so many prophets in the Old Testament were so strong, so bold and sometimes so downright nasty (though they were saying exactly what God wanted them to say!) was because they lived out in the wilderness by themselves. They were lonely. Those prophets walked out of the wilderness angry with the whole world. Now they were prophets! If the Church today doesn't want prophets like that, the best thing they can do is to show a lot of love to those in spiritual leadership.

As in any loving relationship, we must develop our relationship with God through openness and honesty. One of the ways we share intimate fellowship with Him is at His table. The Eucharist is a place of fellowship for us which gives an understanding of godly compassion. But beyond this finite experience of eating and drinking together is a fellowship in the Spirit that the table of the Lord prepares within us. When we partake of the Eucharist at the Lord's table, we are able to discern who we really are in Christ and to enjoy close fellowship with Him through forgiveness and renewal.

We will never manifest the Kingdom of God in our lives until we demonstrate proper love relationships to God and to man. Love for God alone, or love for mankind alone is not the Kingdom mentality that fulfills God's purposes in us. Agape love for God enables us to effectively love others.

201

In illustrating things of the Kingdom of God, Jesus told an interesting story. A banquet was prepared and invitations went out for selected guests to come to the exquisitely prepared table for fellowship. Almost immediately, the invited guests started making excuses: "I have some big deals to take care of this week." "I have to work until 5:30." "I don't have time." We, like the invited guests, sometimes make every kind of excuse to God. People usually manage to do the things which they really commit themselves to do.

The banquet hall was already luxuriously spread. Finally, the host got weary with all the excuses of the invited guests. He told his bewildered servants to forget about the invited guests and to go into the streets and bring all the hungry people to his table. Today God is saying to His people, "My table is spread. Don't miss the feast."

We develop an intimate relationship with God by developing trusting relationships with other people. How can we love God whom we have not seen if we cannot love others? How can we trust God when we are unable to trust one another? How can a Christian be obedient to God's voice and listen to spiritual authority in heaven when he cannot listen to God's direction through established authority on earth? The quality of our relationship with God is contingent upon the love and trust we invest in earthly relationships.

"Not forsaking the assembling of ourselves together . . . and so much the more as you see the Day approaching" (Hebrews 10:25). The vernacular terminology may sound strange, but going to church is keeping "a date" with God and with His people. Some Christians say, "I can serve God in my own way. I can be a 'good Christian' without gathering with God's people in a church." The attitude engendered by such thinking is in total disobedience to God's Word.

How can a Christian claim to be in obedience to God and yet fail to keep God's commandments? When believers seek God together, they create an atmosphere where lasting, trusting relationships develop. The extraordinary power of the early church was born in the upper room when dedicated people were seeking God together. Invincible fellowship is birthed by people who wholeheartedly seek a common cause. The key to Christian growth, both emotionally and spiritually, is when unified Christians seek fellowship with God. We cannot love, serve and fellowship with God if we cannot love, serve and fellowship with other people.

Finally, if we truly want to manifest the Kingdom of God in our relationships, three factors will keep natural and spiritual relationships vibrant and alive. The first factor is true forgiveness. Forgiveness is often misunderstood in its application in our relationships. Forgiveness means actually regarding an offense as if it never occurred. When a person truly forgives, he never even refers to the offense again. Some people actually get angry because God is always willing to forgive. They prefer that God punish someone rather than forgive him.

God said to Jonah, "Go down to Nineveh and tell them I'm going to destroy the people because they will not worship me or follow My plan." When Jonah finally got to Nineveh, he started preaching the message God had sent him to proclaim. He preached the truth so effectively that the whole town put on sackcloth and ashes and repented of their sins. Because of

God's unchangeable character, He forgave them.

Jonah's fury was directed toward God because God forgave the repenting people who heard Jonah's warning. If we do not learn to forgive as God does, our own forgiveness from the Lord is at stake. God's law states, "I will not listen to your prayers if you do not learn how to forgive others. I'll close My ears to you." A person will never escape judgment of his own sins until he learns how to forgive others for their offenses.

The second factor that is essential to natural and spiritual relationships is trust. The Kingdom of God is built in trust combined with love, another important factor. I've heard some people say, "My trust has been destroyed. If I ever recover, I'll need to search for someone whom I can trust." No, discrimination against people is not the basis of trust. Others say, "Well, people have to prove themselves to me before I will ever trust them." That attitude is not the basis of trust either.

I have often trusted people even when I knew they were not going to live up to my trust in them. Even though they would sometimes fail, I knew if I trusted them long enough, they would eventually raise themselves to a level which justified my trusting them. We must trust people even when they are not worthy and trust seems like a foolish risk. If a wife wants a husband she can totally trust, she must keep on trusting him until he reaches the level of her trust. Some families lose their children because they do not trust them. Even when they know their children are making wrong decisions, they should offer their trust again. God trusts us even when we are wrong.

Trust was exemplified in Joseph's believing Mary with

whom he has not been intimate when she said, "But, Joseph, this child is from God." Trust is obedience to the Lord when Joseph said, "Mary, I will not expose you. I'll take care of you." Mary and Joseph's relationship exemplifies spiritual trust in God and in each other.

The time has come when the Church must learn to believe in people by trusting and supporting them. Even when people fail, we need to hold onto them in faith and love and eventually restore them again to a level of trust. If love covers a multitude of sins, how much more should God-like trust cover?

The final, essential factor to natural and spiritual relationships is very important. We should release those closest to us to fulfill their creativity and their God-given potential. Many close relationships die because they are smothered by possessiveness. We must release the fulfillment of God-given abilities in others. Imagine someone suppressing the curiosity in George Washington Carver who took one little peanut and made a vast variety of products. Can you imagine not releasing that kind of creativity? We must learn to appreciate the unlimited potential in our companions and our families and to encourage the release of those abilities. When we hold tight to those we love and smother their talents for fear of losing their affections, we put them into miserable enslavement and captivity.

Sometimes we totally misunderstand God's intentions. God is the God of all creation. He made everything that is good because every good and perfect gift comes from the Father of Light. We must learn how to release ourselves to achieve our own full potential in the Kingdom of God. God desires to develop His people into those who will demonstrate His Kingdom to this world by their lifestyles. Do not be afraid to allow God's development to perfect each individual in the maturing Body of Christ.

Some people get detached from life. They may have the "mind" of God, but they don't have His "heart." I've prayed, "God, I want Your heart." Sometimes we pray only for the mind of Christ when maybe we should first say, "I want the heart of God. I want to feel what Jesus feels." Jesus was moved with compassion. I believe when we finally understand these concepts, God will enlarge our love for Him and for each other. I believe together we can face the real world. We can be sensitive to our real needs, and not only ours, but the needs in others. We will then know when and how to draw the lines properly, and yet recognize the way to move in a spiritual dimension so that God can do His work through us.

God is looking for a people to be His mature Bride. The Bride of Jesus Christ knows not only how to give, but also how to receive love. Many Christians know better how to give love than how to receive it. God leans over the balcony of heaven and says to us, "Church, I want your flowers of love. I want your songs of love to me. I want private hours with you." An intimate, loving relationship with God is the key to understanding man's purpose on planet earth. Whenever we love and serve God's people, we are bringing flowers to God. Flowers? What a sad indictment for Christians if God were to say, "You don't bring Me flowers anymore."

ABOUT THE AUTHOR

Bishop Earl Paulk is senior pastor of Chapel Hill Harvester Church located in Atlanta, Georgia. Chapel Hill Harvester Church has eighteen full-time pastors serving a local parish of over four thousand people with thousands more receiving ministry by television and outreach ministries.

Bishop Paulk grew up in a classical Pentecostal family as the son of Earl P. Paulk Sr., a former assistant general overseer of the Church of God. His grandfather, Elisha Paulk, was a Freewill Baptist preacher.

Personal and educational exposure have given Bishop Paulk an ecumenical understanding enjoyed by few church leaders in the world today. He earned a Bachelor of Arts degree from Furman University which is a Baptist institution, and a Masters of Divinity degree from Candler School of Theology which is a Methodist seminary.

Earl Paulk was named to the office of Bishop in the International Communion of Charismatic Churches in 1982. He assumes oversight of many churches, directly and indirectly influenced by the ministry of Chapel Hill Harvester Church. The church hosts an annual Pastors' Conference in which leaders from local churches across the nation absorb anointed teaching, observe ministry demonstration and have the opportunity for personal dialogue on the major concerns confronting the Church today.

Under Bishop Paulk's leadership, Chapel Hill Harvester Church has become a successful working prototype of a true Kingdom Church. The foundation of the church is Kingdom principles applied to the Biblical concept of a City of Refuge.

The church ministries include a home for unwed mothers; a licensed child placement agency; ministry to those chemically addicted and their families; a ministry to those wishing to come out of the homosexual community; outreach programs to nursing homes, prisons, and home-bound individuals; Alpha, one of the most widely acclaimed youth ministries in the nation; and many other ministries designed to meet the needs of the Body of Christ.

Television outreach includes the **Harvester Hour** and the **K-Dimension** programs seen weekly on P.T.L. Satellite Network and on numerous other television broadcasts nationwide.

Chapel Hill Harvester Church is the tangible expression of God's love through the visionary efforts of Bishop Earl Paulk, his wife, Norma, and founding pastors Don and Clariece Paulk.

Other books by Bishop Earl Paulk:

Early books:

Your Pentecostal Neighbor
Forward in Faith
The Divine Runner

Recent books:

The Wounded Body of Christ
Ultimate Kingdom
Satan Unmasked

Order Form

Qty.	Title	Price	Amount
	BOOKS		
	Satan Unmasked	$7.95	
	Ultimate Kingdom	$5.95	
	Wounded Body of Christ	$3.50	
	Divine Runner	$3.25	
	Sex Is God's Idea	$5.95	
	BOOKLETS		
	Form With Power	$1.00	
	A Must For Every New Convert	$1.00	
	Faith Finished	$1.00	
	The Great Escape Theory	$1.00	
	So Close Yet So Far Away	$1.00	
	Laws Of The Precious Covenant	$1.00	
	The Handwriting On The Wall	$1.00	
	Set For The Defense Of The Gospel	$1.00	
	The Proper Function Of The Church	$1.00	
	Unity Of Faith	$1.00	

☐ Please send me a free catalog of other Books and Teaching Cassettes.

	Amount
Sub-Total	
GA Residents Add 4% Tax	
Shipping & Handling	$2.50
TOTAL	

MAILING ADDRESS

Name _____

Address _____

City _____ State _____ Zip _____

Phone (   ) _____

Mail complete form with payment to:

K Dimension Publishers
P.O. Box 7300
Atlanta, GA 30357

Order Form

Qty.	Title	Price	Amount
	BOOKS		
	Satan Unmasked	$7.95	
	Ultimate Kingdom	$5.95	
	Wounded Body of Christ	$3.50	
	Divine Runner	$3.25	
	Sex Is God's Idea	$5.95	
	BOOKLETS		
	Form With Power	$1.00	
	A Must For Every New Convert	$1.00	
	Faith Finished	$1.00	
	The Great Escape Theory	$1.00	
	So Close Yet So Far Away	$1.00	
	Laws Of The Precious Covenant	$1.00	
	The Handwriting On The Wall	$1.00	
	Set For The Defense Of The Gospel	$1.00	
	The Proper Function Of The Church	$1.00	
	Unity Of Faith	$1.00	

☐ Please send me a free catalog of other Books and Teaching Cassettes.

Sub-Total		
GA Residents Add 4% Tax		
Shipping & Handling		$2.50
TOTAL		

MAILING ADDRESS

Name _____

Address _____

City _____ State _____ Zip _____

Phone ( ) _____

Mail complete form with payment to:

K Dimension Publishers
P.O. Box 7300
Atlanta, GA 30357